D0090440

MICHAEL JACKSON'S

BAR & COCKTAIL COMPANION

MICHAEL JACKSON'S

BAR & COCKTAIL COMPANION

THE CONNOISSEUR'S HANDBOOK

RUNNING PRESS
PHILADELPHIA • LONDON

Published in Great Britain in 1994 by Mitchell Beazley, an imprint of
Octopus Publishing Group Ltd, 2–4 Heron Quays, London E14 4JP

First published 1979 as Michael Jackson's Pocket Bar Book

Reprinted 1979, 1981 (three times), 1983, 1984, 1985, 1987, 1988, 1997, 2004
Revised editions 1984, 1994

9 8 7 6 5 4 3 2 1
Digit on the right indicates the number of this printing
Library of Congress Control Number: 94-73889
ISBN 0-7624-1966-0

A CIP record for this book is available from the British Library.

Editors: Stephanie Horner, Susan Keevil
Art Editor: Paul Tilby
Executive Editor: Anne Ryland
Art Director: Jacqui Small
Photography: Tim Imrie
Production: Michelle Thomas
Printed by Mandarin Offset, Hong Kong

Cover design by Frances J. Soo Ping Chow, Running Press Book Publishers
This book may be ordered by mail from the publisher.
Please include $2.50 for postage and handling.
But try your bookstore first!

Running Press Book Publishers
125 South Twenty-second Street
Philadelphia, Pennsylvania 19103-4399

Visit us on the web!
www.runningpress.com

Guide to symbols

- (g) A generic term
- (p) A proprietary brand
- • Essential to a well-stocked bar
- ★ Standard cocktails
- ♥ Sweet drinks
- Ｙ Short drinks
- ▮ Long drinks

CONTENTS

Pousse-Café *A spectacular production, if it can be done.* *See page 203.*

INTRODUCTION

In most advanced nations, people who enjoy alcoholic beverages are trying to "drink less but better." Or to consume less but taste more. It is a question not only of lifestyle and health but also of the greater pleasure there is to be experienced. We are becoming far more discriminating drinkers. Indiscriminate drinking was always more of a rite than a pleasure.

After the deluge of warnings during the 1980s about the effects of drink on health, some exaggerated and others arguably untrue, the 1990s have brought cooling springs of common sense. Various well-publicized studies have suggested that alcohol may reduce the appetite for more fattening products, and can aid digestion; that red wine in particular may help combat ailments ranging from gallstones to heart disease, cancer and radiation sickness; that beer counters the common cold – and some of the effects of aging; that whisky lowers blood pressure; even that the Bloody Mary may help victims of arthritis. No one is suggesting champagne for breakfast every morning, though on a special occasion a couple of *flûtes* with the scrambled eggs and smoked salmon might brighten the day. The more restrained might add orange juice or peach to make a Buck's Fizz, Mimosa or Bellini. Italians or French are as likely to warm a cold, early morning with a coffee and fruit brandy.

The travel-weary know the pleasure of a midmorning Bloody Mary on the plane, the alcohol as a relaxant and tomato juice for energizing sugar and vitamins (and, of course, that protection against arthritis caused by shortage of legroom). It may not be explained this way at the time, but can be post-rationalized. In Bavaria, it is a midmorning wheat beer with a veal sausage, especially after church on Sunday.

No true Italian or Frenchperson would entertain lunch without wine, while Germans and Belgians may additionally require beer. Thankfully, neither taste has yet been harmonized by the European Union.

An Italian or French vermouth, or a fino sherry, before dinner? One of the lighter, drier Scotches, or a chilled aquavit? A proper London Dry gin-based Martini? Some diners espouse wine throughout, perhaps finishing with Sauternes or sweet sherry or port. Others take armagnac, cognac or calvados as a digestif. Or a sherry-aged Speyside whisky. It surely has to be a Scotch, a smoky Islay malt, with a book at bedtime.

The art of civilized drinking rests on mood, time and place. Which, where and when? These questions here elicit a pocketful of information, and an idea or two, in concise form for easy reference, for the professional and amateur bartender alike, and for the traveller.

Whence came the great drinks, and to what ingredients and patient procedures does each owe its character? How are they served to best advantage? Will they marry happily? Should they be stirred or shaken?

There are more mixed drinks than can ever be digested, but a selection of around 250 allows for most occasions and a great many constituents. Ingredients include patent aperitifs, vermouths, wines fortified and otherwise, spirits, liqueurs or cordials, and beers. Not only are the major types and styles detailed in this book, but also a good many lesser-known examples to tickle the palate or imagination.

To explore the world's local bars is to enjoy a thousand flavors. An educated palate does not work part-time. Those who stick to the same drink for life are engaging not so much in monogamy as in masochism.

FANCY FREE *AN EXCELLENT COCKTAIL USING RYE WHISKEY.* *SEE PAGE 169.*

TRAVEL AND DRINK

Drink has enjoyed a long and happy marriage with travel since the days when pilgrims broke their footsore journeys at abbeys for refreshment, sowing the seeds for Trappist beer, Benedictine, Chartreuse and many other monastic delights. Had it not been for that early tourist Marco Polo, and the spicy souvenirs he brought home, Italian aperitifs would have a less interesting flavor. If Christopher Columbus had not made his business trip to the West Indies, taking sugar cane with him, the Caribbean would not be famous for rum.

Travel is not for feet, or bottoms strapped into the airplane seat; it is for the eyes, the mind, and most of all for the palate.

It is a two-way street, of course. The Londoner visiting Paris and ordering a Pernod may find *le scotch* being urged upon him as the height of chic. Outside the ungrateful English-speaking world, Scotch is almost universally the most valued drink. The American, carefully Gucci-shod and seeking the authentic grappa in Rome, may be smilingly offered Coca-Cola by someone wearing sneakers. To accept would be worse than staying at home.

Nor has a country been properly visited unless a bottle or two is brought home. It may turn out to be available at the liquor store round the corner, but only the brandy which was actually bought in Spain will evoke the dust of a bullring; only the aquavit procured in Norway or Denmark will properly accompany a snack of marinated herrings. The more authentic the drink, the more obscure and elusive it may prove to be, but half the fun lies in the chase, and the other half in the acquisition of the taste for the stuff.

The pleasures of life were never intended to be obtained easily, and it is always necessary to know the rules of the game, even in your own country. These rules may vary, too, within a single country, and they invariably do so between the cosmopolitan cities and the industrial or rural regions. Both the American continent and Europe divide laterally in their drinking styles, though the change is made clearer by the Mexican frontier than by the Rhine.

In each continent it is the northern countries where restrictions are to be found, with the inevitable reprisal of determined and often furtive drinking. It is a matter not only of religious influence, Protestant as against Catholic, but also of climate and mealtimes.

In the cold countries of Europe (for example, Scotland, the Nordic lands, Poland and Russia) spirits offer at least the illusion of warmth. Then, still using grain, especially barley, is the beer belt (England, Belgium, Germany, and the Czech Republic). A vestigial belt of cider districts separates this from the warmer, grape-growing countries (principally Portugal, Spain, France, Italy, and the Balkans). This is a question of emphasis rather than clear-cut borders. Most countries have at least one spirit, virtually all make beer, and many have wines.

Most of the world's best-known alcoholic drinks assumed their modern form in Europe, though the arts of fermentation and distillation were probably first practiced by the ancient civilizations of the East. Beyond the Balkans, Georgia, and Armenia, traditions of wine, *anis*-flavored drinks and brandies are to some extent staunched by Islam. In several Middle Eastern and Asian countries, brandies made from dates or coconut sap are known as arak (spellings vary).

Regional and national drinks are influenced by the materials available (though this may not explain the Chinese predilection for putting lizards into bottles). At a Japanese meal, rice "wine" (sake) may be served alongside beer, wine and local or Scotch whisky. Contrary to rumor, Japan's own whiskies are impeccably well-made.

Some highlights and guidelines for the international traveller follow.

THE AMERICAS

CANADA

The Quebecois, many of whom originate from coastal northern France, still have a vestigial taste for sweet liqueurs, and *jenever* (perhaps rendered *genever*) gins might be found in the province. The male dominance of drinking places lingers, too, in Quebec and in some of the more frontier-ish towns and cities in other provinces and territories. Some taverns and "beverage rooms" can be very basic indeed, and restrictions vary from one county to the next. Scottish settlement, especially in Ontario, brought its own Protestant rigor and gave Canada its own, rye-tinged, whisky. Liquor stores are run by the provinces (like the state stores across the frontier in some northerly parts of the U.S.), but their joyless design is being softened, especially in the bigger cities. In Toronto, as in many of the world's most cosmopolitan cities, Italian influence makes for sunnier drinking and dining, and Vancouver is spiced by Asian immigrants.

THE UNITED STATES

Puritans were the founding fathers, but their country became the land of conspicuous consumption. This ambivalence is still evident. On the one hand, the U.S. has legislators who would treat alcohol like a hard drug; some severe restrictions (it is possible to be arrested for drinking from a bottle or can on the street); a minimum age of 21; some suicidally gloomy "set 'em up, Joe" bars; and a strident Prohibitionist lobby. On the other hand, lavish advertisements promoting drinks are everywhere, measures of spirits are perilously generous, and bartenders in even modest restaurants are especially adept with that American invention, the cocktail.

America's first spirit, New England rum, is no longer produced. For a time, Bourbon whiskey was a threatened species, but high-quality "small batch" bottlings are helping win it the respect it has always deserved. Tennessee whiskey is easy to find, straight rye harder. Applejack has become esoteric, but fruit brandies are now being made in California and the Pacific Northwest. That region's wines are rightly renowned, but it is also becoming famous for its (typically, very hoppy) microbrewed beers. There are more than 400 microbreweries and brew pubs throughout the United States.

The drinker will have a fine time in northern, coastal cities, like Seattle and San Francisco, Boston and Baltimore, and in insouciant Chicago or lusty New Orleans; small-town America, some of the hotter states, and the Bible Belt hold less promise.

MEXICO

The most famous spirit of Mexico, tequila, is made principally around the village and dormant volcano of that name, near Guadalajara in the Jalisco province. It is produced from the bulbous root, or heart, of the

"Tequilana," "blue," or "Weber" (after the botanist who identified it) variety of the agave plant. The agave, also known as the maguey or mezcal, is a cactus-like plant related to the lily. Elsewhere in Mexico, especially in Oaxaca, other regional varieties of the plant are used to produce a more basic spirit known as mezcal. Some bottles contain the pickled corpse of a grub that feeds off the agave. The drinker who swallows the grub is held to have enhanced his potency. Mezcal is often served from plastic jerricans.

Pulque is a strong (up to about 10% alcohol by volume) fermented drink, made from the agave. It is milky in color, sherbety in taste, and not unlike "traditional beers" made in developing nations. It is served from open roadside stalls, and at *pulquerias*, especially in the area of Mexico City.

Macho Mexicans like to submerge a glass of tequila in their beer; this *submarino*, a counterpart to the American "boilermaker," is one of many tequila-based mixed drinks. Young tourists tend to be keen on the tequila "slammer," topped off with lime juice and sometimes sparkling wine. This is slammed on the bar-counter to enhance its sparkle.

There is a huge range of fruit juices (*jugos*), iced shakes (*liquados*), and flavored waters (*aquas frescas*) available from street stalls.

Unfortunately, Mexico's brewing industry has become known to the outside world for bland, corn-tasting beers like Corona and Sol. The country's breweries do have more interesting products, such as the Pilsner-style Bohemia, the Vienna-style Dos Equis, the darker Negra Modelo and the Christmas seasonal Nochebuena.

Drinking in bars, or the often male-oriented cantina, is usually accompanied by snacks, known as *botana*, perhaps one of the many variations on the tortilla theme. Lunch and dinner are eaten late, and the bars are open from midday to midnight or later.

THE CARIBBEAN

Rums vary in style from one island to the next, and go into fresh-tasting, exotic cocktails made with pineapple, mango, banana, melon and other tropical fruits. Cocktail ingredients like Angostura bitters, curaçao, falernum and orgeat all have Caribbean origins. So does the Daiquiri cocktail, devised in Cuba. In addition to light lager beers, some islands have dark examples and strong stouts.

The Caribbean is the land of late-night drinking at cold-supper shops. Customs vary, but favorite supper snacks include, not surprisingly, fresh, salted, and pickled fish, beef and pork with an endless variety of hot sauces, and cassava bread, known on many islands as *bammie*.

CENTRAL AND SOUTH AMERICA

There is the odd spirit similar to mezcal and many local names for variants on rums and brandies (including some of the marc/grappa type), depending upon the local crop. In Colombia and Ecuador, rum is often flavored with aniseed. In several countries, spirits are often served with chocolate drinks or coffee.

Peru, Chile and Bolivia have versions of the Muscat brandy pisco. Brazil uses sugar in its Dreher brandy, and has a variation on white rum called cachaça (or caxaca). A similar drink called caña is found in Uruguay and Argentina. The latter country, with its Italian influence, also has its vermouths.

Drinking places vary from the basic cantina to fashionable cafés in big cities, and in Argentina the Italian-style bar that serves aperitifs, meaty sandwiches, iced confections, pastries and digestifs.

Throughout the continent, drinks often come with snacks, variously known as *bacaditos, antojitos, boquillas, fritangas, tadapados,* and *salgadinhos*. These may manifest themselves as toasted corn, fried chick-peas, potato dishes, plantain, banana and yucca.

EUROPE

THE BRITISH ISLES

One of the best recent developments has been the growing number of Scotch whisky distilleries that offer tours, tastings, and an opportunity to buy the product on the premises. Hotel bars and pubs (the latter more common in southern cities like Edinburgh and Glasgow) have begun to stock much wider ranges of the native spirit, and there is a growing number of speciality shops.

Scotland now has more liberal and flexible licensing hours than England and Wales, though the latter's once awkward opening (closing?) practices have been greatly relaxed. In England, pubs are permitted (but not obliged) to open from 11 in the morning, and must call last orders before 11 in the evening. There has continued to be a period of closure on Sunday afternoons between 3 and 7 but even that is set to vanish. In Wales, some districts have Sunday closing. In Northern Ireland, pubs do not open until 11:30 a.m. and have short Sunday hours (12:30–2:30 p.m.; 7:00–10:00 p.m.). In the Republic, they open from 10:30 a.m. to 11:30 p.m., but on Sundays close between 2 and 4 in the afternoon.

In line with the European Union, the miserably small standard measure of spirit in Britain has been increased to 25 milliliters (just over three-quarters of an American fluid ounce). A "double," however, is only 35 milliliters – less than before.

Visitors to Britain who want to spoil their Scotch with ice are advised to ask for it (the odd purist barman has been known to demur, though the young even add lemonade). An order for "A Martini" may yield only the Italian vermouth of that name; to be sure, ask for a "Dry Martini Cocktail." Gin is England's native spirit, often ordered with tonic water as a summer refresher. The traditional "pink gin" (with Angostura bitters) is, sadly, rarely seen.

British Prime Minister John Major evoked "warm beer" as a national icon. Traditional, cask-conditioned, ales are kept at a cellar temperature in the lower to mid-50s Fahrenheit (hardly "warm") because they would never reach maturity if chilled. At this temperature, a British ale expresses its full flavor and offers a soothing, sociable, pint.

In a true English local, any bar snacks are so unpleasant as to discourage eating ("scratchings" of pork skin being a prime example). With legislation to loosen brewers' control of pubs, many are now entertaining gastronomic adventures, ranging from cardboardy lasagne to "international cuisine" to, in some, seriously good food.

THE NORDIC COUNTRIES

Iceland has in recent years ceased to be officially "dry," but, like Norway and Sweden, still has very high prices and many restrictions, due to religious and political pressures. Those Nordic countries that join the European Union will have to ease their legislation on drink, and Finland has already done so, to some extent.

Long before the religious constraints, most Nordic countries had traditions of farmhouse brewing and (illegal) distilling. Viking images are evoked by the farmhouse brewers of Norway and Sweden, who use juniper twigs and berries in addition to hops. A similar tradition in Finland and Estonia, sometimes employing rye, is a part of sauna culture: sweat first, then sit half-naked by the lake drinking the beer. The Finns have a special name for this beverage – *sahti* – while the Estonians simply refer to it as home-brew.

All of these countries have modern brewing industries, some making strong Imperial Stouts as well as a variety of lager styles. Denmark, which has far more liberal laws on drink, boasts a considerable brewing history, and played an important role in perfecting the lager method.

The Finns make sparkling wines from the whitecurrant (*valkoherukka*), among which one, called Kavaljeeri, is produced by the same method as champagne. Wines, liqueurs and flavored vodkas are made from a variety of northern berries. These include the cloudberry (*lakka*), Arctic bramble (*mesimarja*) and buckthorn (*tyrni*). Denmark has its famous cherry "brandy" (actually, a liqueur), made by the Heering family.

Basic spirits, often made from potatoes or beets, or from barley, are usually known as *brännvin* ("brandy") in Sweden, *acquavit* or *akvavit* ("water of life") in Norway and Denmark, *viina* in Finland, and vodka in several countries. These drinks are usually consumed cold, often in one swallow, as in the Slavic countries, and frequently accompanied by snacks of dried or pickled fish.

Aquavit is usually flavored with caraway, and sometimes with dill, arrowroot and other plants. Other exotic ingredients, including coriander, star aniseed and grains of paradise, testify to the Northerners' maritime history. Linie Aquavit (see page 40) gains in maturity by taking a sea voyage across the equator. The Swedes have a bottled "punch" inspired by the rum-like arak of Indonesia, and the Danes flavor one aquavit with madeira.

The Estonians use rum essence, oil of Cyprus orange and cinnamon to produce a liqueur called Old Tallinn (named after the capital city). Among their many liqueurs, perhaps the oddest is one called Cock on a Tree Stump. It is said to make the drinker crow like a cockerel. The drink is flavored with citrus essence and caraway, and the bottle contains a rock of candy-sugar. This rock causes the sugar already dissolved in the liqueur to crystalize, thus making the drink drier and stronger. If the bottle is kept too long, the growing crystalization breaks the glass. Such eccentricities abound in the European liqueur houses, in port cities all the way from Tallinn and Gdansk to Amsterdam and Antwerp.

THE NETHERLANDS

The Dutch "brown café," wood-panelled and smoked-stained, is first cousin of the English pub, though it remains open longer. Like the pub, it is a place in which to drink and talk, and not to eat, though bar snacks are served. Traditionally, these have been cubes of cheese or sausage; the curiously named "bitter balls," made from a veal roux in bread crumbs or Indonesian-style *sate* (meat on skewers, with a spicy peanut sauce) with wedges of bread, but more elaborate snacks have appeared in recent years. When people entertain at home, excessively tenacious guests are sent on their way with a final snack, a "Thrower Out" (*uitsmijter*), which is comprised of two fried eggs on ham-covered bread.

In recent years, the Netherlanders have become pioneers of the speciality beer café, offering a huge range of brews, some from the southern brewing provinces of Dutch Brabant and Limburg, and many from neighboring Belgium.

Historically, the Catholic south is most associated with beer and *joie de vivre*, the Protestant north with jenever gin and, allegedly, secret drinking. Amsterdam has a tradition of liqueurs and fruit "brandies," and one or two bars specializing in these products. Friesland has a famous herbal bitters called Beerenburg.

A glass of jenever makes a fine appetizer for a salted herring or a bread-roll (*broodje*) filled with pickled meat or steak tartare.

BELGIUM

The world's most distinctive beers are Belgium's great gift to the drinker, though for years he or she seemed unaware of this.

Among beer-lovers, Belgium is especially known for the Lambic family of beers, made on the rural outskirts of Brussels. These beers are characterized by a wineyness imparted by wild yeasts. "Straight" Lambic, which is almost still, is hard to find outside the region, but a sparkling blend of young and old "vintages," called Gueuze, is more readily available. These are the beers with which to steam (and consume) the famous mussels of Belgium. Lambics are also often used as a basis for fruit beers, traditionally cherry *kriek* and raspberry *frambozen* (in Flemish) or *framboise* (in French). The sweet-and-sour reddish-brown ales made further west also serve as both ingredient in and accompaniment to the national stew, the Carbonade Flamande.

Belgium has countless stronger ales, some reaching 12 percent, among them several made in Trappist monasteries (five have their own breweries, and there is a sixth across the Dutch border).

One reason for the popularity of very strong beers was the prohibition for many years on the serving of spirits in cafés. This law has now been repealed, and there are several cafés specializing in the many and distinctive Belgian versions of *jenever*.

Belgium has probably more drinking-places per head than any other country. Most of these are cafés, which can have very varied opening hours, and are likely to serve only limited bar-snacks. There are also specialist beer-bars, some of which serve *cuisine à la bière*. At its most modest interpretation, this means dishes that are thought to be well-suited to beer. More often, it indicates the use of carefully chosen beers in original dishes.

This is a country in which eating and drinking are of the utmost importance, and meals are taken at great leisure. There are more Michelin-starred restaurants per head than in France, and the Belgians are major importers of fine wines.

THE GERMAN-SPEAKING WORLD

Germany itself, the nation with the most breweries by far (about 1,200) is also a major winegrower and producer of fruit brandies and grain-based spirits.

The German term Schnapps can indicate almost any short drink, usually a spirit, and most often a clear one based on grain. More often, this is ordered simply as Korn. This drink and the closely related Steinhäger or Wacholder gin are most often seen in the north. The former East Germany also has a taste for clear, grain-based, spirits.

Obstler (fruit) brandies, often made from pears or apples, or both, are widely available. So are Kirsch variations, and distillates from several other fruits. There are also many liqueurs flavored with flowers or roots, such as Enzian (gentian). These products are especially popular in the south, and straddle the borders with France, Switzerland and Austria.

Frankfurt and some parts of Switzerland have Apfelwein, a hard cider, while the Rhineland, Baden-Württemberg and Franconia have a wide range of grape wines. Their traditional wines are medium-sweet whites, and it is not unusual for these to be served at the end of the meal, the main course having been washed down with beer. Drier wines, more suitable to accompany meals, are also now beginning to make an impact.

In Bavaria, a cloudy, fruity-tasting Weizenbier or Weissbier (both terms mean wheat beer) may be taken with a midmorning *Brotzeit* (a bread-based "second breakfast"), featuring a pair of *Weisswurst* (veal sausages). This is never served after noon. A Pilsner may be treated as an aperitif before lunch or dinner. A less dry export-style beer, a style originating from Dortmund, might accompany a summer picnic (heavily featuring large black radishes) in a beer garden. A stronger Bockbier, often dark, sustains Bavarians in cooler weather. If the season is cold, the beer will be enjoyed under the Gothic vaulting of a beer-hall. Kölsch (the lightly fruity golden ale of Cologne) or Altbier (the darker counterpart found especially in Düsseldorf) are more likely to be found in a cosier, often crowded, tavern.

Both wine and beer, according to the region, provide the focus for endless village festivals. Germany uses several different names for drinking places. A Gasthaus implies an inn, though not all have bedrooms; a Wirtschaft or Wirthaus can be any type of drinking place; a Pinte is a rough, simple, establishment; a Kneipe tends to have a studenty ambience; a Destille is, in the parlance of Berlin, a hard-drinking joint. Most of these places open around midday for about 12 hours. Many have a Ruhetag (a rest day, when they are closed), often on Mondays.

Beer and other drinks are also served in the Konditorei, the German counterpart to a French pâtisserie. Beer is less evident, but aperitifs and brandies may be found in similar establishments across the various southern borders, especially in Austria.

Many of Germany's drinking traditions occur in modified forms in Alsace (northeastern France), Switzerland and the one-time Austrian Empire (including the Czech Republic and some other former Eastern Bloc regions). Anyone who has ever enjoyed a German beer-garden might also appreciate the serving of young wine in the mock-rustic Buschenschenk or Heurige of Austria.

FRANCE

The country of the café. The price of your drink ascends as you move from the bar stool to the table, to the terrace. The question is not only where to drink but also what to drink, with such an embarrassment of choice. Wine may be drunk at any time, by the glass if so desired, but is primarily ordered with meals. A French worker may have half a liter with his lunch, rounded off with coffee and calvados.

Of the brandies, calvados, cognac, and armagnac are produced in rigidly demarcated areas, but the *eaux-de-vie* of Alsace are not, and they straddle the frontier of Switzerland and Germany. The marc type of brandy is produced everywhere, but with special pride in Burgundy.

Kir, a mix of white wine and blackcurrant liqueur which originates from Burgundy, is a popular aperitif thoughout France. The same is true of vermouths and patent aperitifs which tend to come from a loosely defined area around the Alps. Like Pernod, pastis is a national drink: the connoisseur asks for it by brand name.

A surprisingly large amount of beer is drunk in France, especially in the summer. Most is of the bottom-fermented type, mainly from Alsace, but some interesting top-fermented beers are made in the northeast.

France is very much of the southern school, with drinking usually related to eating. Though restaurants may serve casual drinkers on the terrace, cafés rarely provide more than a sandwich: cheese, ham or pâté.

SPAIN

In no country does the grape display a greater virtuosity: the wine-based punch called sangria as a cooler at the beach; fino sherry with snacks; amontillado and montilla or sparkling cava as an aperitif; wine as a casual drink and with meals, from a communal skin *bota* in the north or a glass *porrón* in Catalonia; Málaga, Tarragona and the richer sherries as dessert wines; brandies as digestifs and as hard liquor.

Spanish bars may be dark, narrow rooms with just enough space for a row of bar stools, or they may be bright and noisy, with a bullfight or football on the TV in the corner; amazingly, they are nearly always cool havens in summer.

The delight of Spanish drinking is the range of accompanying snacks, known as *tapas*. These vary from such simple pleasures as the ham or spicy sausage hanging above the bar to a whole array of prepared dishes, two or three of which make a meal in themselves: thick Spanish omelets; various types of olives; roasted nuts; potato, bean and chick-pea salads; mushrooms, kidneys, prawns, squid, and many other varieties of seafood, either sautéed with garlic or simmered in rich sauces.

The Spanish eat late – lunch between 2:00 and 4:00 p.m. and dinner between 9:00 p.m. and midnight – but there is always a snack and a drink available to keep them going between meals. Allowing for an after-dinner digestif – either brandy or one of the native liqueurs such as Calisay and Cuarenta y Tres – cafés close between midnight and 1:00 a.m. in the country; in cities and seaside resorts, they may remain open until 2:00 a.m. or later.

PORTUGAL

Most port goes overseas, and the little that is left is apt to be reserved for special occasions, although white port is sometimes drunk as an aperitif. Portugal also produces a very varied range of table wines, among which Vinhos Verdes are well-regarded locally. A noted Moscatel is produced at Setúbal.

Aguardente, meaning brandy, and bagaceira, the Portuguese version of marc or grappa, are often consumed with black coffee. There is also a rare eau-de-vie called medronho, made from arbutus berries.

Liqueurs may be served at any time of the day, with small cakes or nuts; the best-known are ginjinha, made from cherries, and beirão, brandy flavored with herbs and spices.

Bars are a city institution; cafés are found everywhere and remain open into the night according to local demand. Snacks may be limited to a bowl of nuts, or may run to steak sandwiches, deep-fried fish or meat pasties, salt cod croquettes, snails, quails, quince marmalade (perhaps served with cheese), and a wide range of pastries, notably tiny glazed custard creams.

CHOCOLATE COCKTAIL *THE INSPIRATION OF HARRY CRADDOCK.* *SEE PAGE 153.*

ITALY

At its borders with Austria and Switzerland, Italy can be a surprisingly cold country. Some bars there open at 6 or 7 in the morning to provide outdoor workers with grappa and coffee to start the day. When served in the same cup this is known as a *caffè corretto*, and it is drunk at any time. Coffee, with or without grappa, is the ubiquitous drink of Italy.

A sign of past Austrian influence in the northern cities is the fancy pâtisserie, which also serves ice-creams, a few savories, coffee, and late-afternoon aperitifs. It is the custom in these establishments to order from the cashier, pay, obtain a receipt and pass that to the waiter so that he knows what to bring. The pâtisserie closes early in the evening, but ordinary cafés and bars stay open until 11, midnight or later.

Even so, the Italians do not customarily drink for drinking's sake. Wine, which Italy produces in enormous quantity and variety, is mainly reserved for mealtimes: interminable lunches and equally gargantuan dinners, starting around 8 in the north and 9:30 in the south.

Cafés and bars are also visited during *la passagiata*, the early evening stroll, when drinking is perhaps the least important part of the ritual of seeing and being seen, with families, friends, and lovers.

The northwest, particularly Genoa and Turin, is Italy's heartland of herbal bitters and vermouths. In the northeast some maraschino-makers hopped across the border into Italy from Dalmatia, in the former Yugoslavia, after World War II.

GREECE

The Greeks do not drink heavily, nor do they like to take alcohol without food. The Greek equivalent to the pub or café is the taverna or *kafeneion*; it may open only in the evenings, especially in small villages. During the week it is a male haunt, with snacks of olives, cheese, and *souvlakia* (grilled pieces of marinated lamb) to accompany beer and ouzo. At weekends the taverna welcomes the whole family to heartier grills and stews, with retsina and other Greek wines to drink, and digestifs of mastika or local orange liqueurs.

Ouzo, known in some places as douzico and in others as raki, is both a casual drink and an aperitif. It is usually diluted with water. A glass of water and some fruit or jam are often provided as a gesture of hospitality, and should never be left untouched.

SERVING DRINKS

Anyone can mix a drink for a friend or two. To serve aperitifs for a dozen dinner guests, or cocktails for 50 people at a party, takes a little more organization. The coward's way out is to hire a bartender but, as always in life, bravery is more fulfilling. Surely the host who enjoys an interesting drink will want to provide a personal touch for the guests?

How, though, to mix Martinis while stirring a little conversation? It must all happen in the same room, with no dashing back and forth to the kitchen while yet more guests arrive. Whatever the protestations of the cramped Manhattan apartment dweller or the determinedly unvulgar English party-giver, there is a lot to be said for having a bar in the home.

It needn't be a shrine for conspicuous consumption, a pocket Ritz, or a monument to bad taste. It may simply be a cocktail cabinet that has fold-out work surfaces, some Deco delight fit for Noel Coward's *Design for Living*; a sturdy trolley with a shelf or two; or a wall unit with a handy recess for a refrigerator. But the need for ice, and plenty of it, a roomy, sturdy, hard-wearing surface, and a double sink for washing and rinsing, all argue the case for a purpose-built bar, even if its utilitarian quality is masked in a tireless extravaganza of pine, bamboo, or ostrich feathers.

Vermouths and patent aperitifs taste better if they are kept lightly chilled; white wines should be kept cold, as should dry sherries; but only aquavits and Slavic vodkas need intense refrigeration. If cocktail glasses are kept in the refrigerator, they will have a stylish frostiness when filled.

A shelf under the counter, but not too low, can house the most frequently used base spirits, a bottle each of dry and sweet vermouth, bitters, soda, and jugs of fruit juices. This way, the bartender does not have to turn his or her back on guests too often. For the same reason, the bar should be a simple, unfussy shape and every drink and piece of equipment should have its regular place to which it is returned immediately after use. It may be tedious to be so methodical, but it saves undignified scrambles, as any professional bartender will testify.

THE BARTENDER'S TOOLS

A lemon-squeezer or juice-extractor of one sort or another is vital. No particular design can be elected as the best, since it is a matter of personal taste as to which handles most easily and extracts the juice most efficiently, but the choice of this simple piece of equipment bears careful consideration. If there are to be many guests, squeeze plenty of juice beforehand for mixed drinks, but not so far in advance that it loses its freshness.

Ice containers come in innumerable designs, most of them aesthetically offensive. Look for capacity and efficient insulation, and have a spare one so that guests can help themselves. If white wines or champagne are to be served, a bucket ice-container in which they can be cooled will also be required.

Tongs are more efficient than a spoon when ice is to be put into a glass, and they don't carry any unwanted water.

Ice crushers come in various designs. Crushed ice (sometimes it is described as being shaved) is required for frappé drinks, Daiquiris and a variety of other treats. Crushers can usually be adjusted to produce cracked ice for drinks like the Old Fashioned. Otherwise, wrap cubes in a towel and crack them with a kitchen mallet. If drinks are mixed in an electric blender, whole ice cubes will damage the blades, but this problem does not arise with mixers made especially for bars.

Jugs for iced water or fruit juice should have an involuted pourer which will hold back the cubes. This type of jug can also be used as a mixing glass, with no need for a strainer.

A scoop is needed to load crushed or cracked ice into a drink, mixing glass or shaker.

The Bartender's Friend is an all-in-one device that opens corked or crown-topped bottles, and cans. It is a handy back-up even if a more elaborate corkscrew is preferred and a bottle-opener is permanently fixed to the bar.

Measures. Each side of the Atlantic has its own variation on the fluid ounce, and the gill, with the centiliter offering yet a fifth system of measurement. So long as all ingredients are measured by the same means, it doesn't matter which of these scales is used. Since more classic cocktails originate from the Americas, the "jigger" used in bars in the United States is a common basic measurement in recipes. A jigger, a term which is sometimes used by "mixologists," contains 1½ U.S. ounces.

Bitters bottles are fitted with caps like those used to pour vinegar or salad oil. This means that a "dash" of Angostura or orange bitters can be shaken out without the need for measurement.

Mixing glasses come in various shapes and sizes, but they are always big enough for the preparation of several drinks at once. The mixing glass, sometimes known as a bar glass, is for drinks that are to be stirred, not shaken. These are drinks that are intended to be clear, not cloudy, and which would be particularly harmed by the greater dilution which is caused by shaking. After being stirred, the drink should be strained into a cocktail glass straight up, or onto fresh ice in a larger glass.

Cocktail Equipment *THE RIGHT TOOLS ARE NOT VITAL, BUT MAKE THE TASK EASIER.*

Muddlers also come in various sizes: large ones for use with a mixing glass, smaller for the drinker's own amusement. They have a bulbous end and are intended for crushing sugar and pounding mint in a drink. A similar device with a paddle-like end is called a swizzle-stick. The shaft is rubbed between the palms of the hands so that the paddle agitates the drink. This trick is intended to calm over-excited drinks and enliven flat ones, but has little useful effect in either case. Still, a swizzle-stick has a harmless decorative value.

Strainers. Classically made by the firm of Hawthorne, its name spelled out in holes. A popular type clips onto the mixing glass.

A bar spoon is used to stir drinks in a mixing glass, or after serving. The "wrong" end can be used as a muddler.

A shaker is used in drinks that contain fruit juices, syrups, very thick liqueurs, or any ingredients that demand a thorough mix. Because the ice gets knocked about in the mixer, there may be considerable dilution, and a clear drink cannot easily be produced. A shaker of classic design incorporates a strainer in the topmost chamber. This simplifies the serving of drinks. A Boston shaker, comprised one half metal and the other half glass, is easier to break open but less convenient in the pouring, since a separate strainer is required.

Paring knife and board. All too easy to forget, yet obviously necessary. How else could one produce with efficiency slivers and twists of lemon or cucumber peel, and slices of orange, which are crisp, clean, and handsome?

USEFUL GLASSES

Ballon

The most versatile glass of all. Ostensibly for red wine, though its size emphasizes the rule of half-filling (or less) for both bouquet and sobriety. Pink patent aperitifs best express their cool and colorful character atop the stem of a well-rounded ballon, with plenty of room to swish the ice around and contemplate a sunny slice of orange. It will even hold a half-pint of beer, though a straight glass is more macho. Approx. 10 oz.

Champagne

The narrow *flûte* glass is preferable, not only on aesthetic grounds but also because it retains the sparkle better. The traditional saucer was intended to cope with the dunking of madeira cake. It can also accommodate a garnish on a champagne cocktail better than the *flûte*.

Cocktail

Essential, elegant, and neatly proportioned. A stem just long enough to protect the small conical bowl from the warmth of the hand. The opening is sufficiently wide to display a garnish. Max. 4 oz.

Collins

For long drinks. The taller the better. Always narrow, often with perfectly straight sides. 10 oz.

Highball

An intermediate size which can serve several purposes. 8 oz.

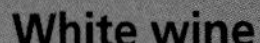

White wine
A long stem so that the hand does not warm the drink. A tall, narrow bowl to retain the cold. A fine line for a delicate wine.

Sherry (not shown)
Those tall schooners are stilted and lumpy and do not hold the bouquet. A dry sherry in a large glass warms before it is drunk. Better to have a small glass which can be refilled from a cooled bottle. The classic glass is the tall, narrow, copita, which closes towards the rim to retain the bouquet. Say 2 oz.

Snifter
The traditional brandy glass, well-rounded to be warmed in the palm of the hand, with a short stem. The rim turns in to hold the powerful bouquet. Enormous glasses look silly.

Liqueur
Rich, sweet liqueurs are served in small quantities. 1–2 oz.

Old Fashioned
For any cocktail served on the rocks. Also doubles for whisky, though the typically chunky Old Fashioned glass is less attractive for that purpose than the cut crystal and faintly tapered tumbler traditionally used for Scotch. 6 oz.

Pousse-café (not shown)
A tall, narrow liqueur glass for this stripy production (see page 203).

Sour

A stemmed glass for a drink which is not strictly a cocktail but isn't long, either. A similar glass is sometimes used for a Fizz. 5–6 oz.

Toddy (not shown)

Heat-proof glasses with handles are useful for hot drinks.

Red wine

Solid looking, to match the fatness of a burgundy or claret, with a shortish stem and a well-rounded bowl to be embraced warmly. The rim should be wide enough to let the wine breathe.

THE A-Z OF DRINKS

For obvious reasons, companies producing drinks like to promote their brand names. This can be confusing for the drinker.

Ask a bartender for a single malt and he may be unable to identify on his shelves the bottle that fits the category. He may require you to order a brand. (Glenfiddich or The Glenlivet, for example, are single malts; Chivas Regal or Johnnie Walker Black are deluxe blended Scotches.)

Every drinker knows Jim Beam, but what is it? (A straight bourbon whiskey from Kentucky.) What is Bacardi? (A white rum.) What is Cointreau? (A company that makes many fruit-based drinks but is known for its *triple sec*, a variety of curaçao orange liqueur.)

Thousands of names are used to identify drinks. Some of the best known, and several rarer ones, are defined here. Proprietary brands are marked (p) and generic terms (g). Cross-references are indicated in bold type. As most of the world is moving to show alcohol as a percentage of volume, that system is used. However, strengths may vary according to local law or custom. The figure for American proof equals twice the alcohol by volume.

If a drink is marked ●, it should be available in a well-stocked bar.

ABRICOTINE (P) 30–35%

Sweet, apricot-flavored after-dinner liqueur based on brandy. From the French liqueur house of Garnier. See also **Apry** and **Apricot brandy**.

MAI-TAI *DECORATIVE AND DELICIOUS, AND NOW A CLASSIC COCKTAIL, BASED ON RUM AND TROPICAL FRUITS.* *SEE PAGE 191.*

ABSINTHE (g) 68%

The Green Muse, because it inspired Hemingway and seduced the brushes of Degas, Toulouse-Lautrec, and Picasso. The Green Goddess for its questionably aphrodisiac qualities. Home-produced illicitly in its native Switzerland and in a legal version in Spain, but banned in most countries since the turn of the century, on now questionable evidence that it endangered health. Its eponymous ingredient wormwood (*Artemisia absinthium*) was blamed for madness and death. Absinthe was replaced by dry *anis* drinks of around 45%, typified by **Pernod**. See also **Pastis**, in which licorice is the prominent ingredient. Both are drunk as hard liquors, especially in Provence, and as aperitifs throughout France. A wide variety of similar-tasting liqueurs is made in Europe by the infusion in neutral spirits of aniseed, licorice, fennel, and other plants.

ACQUAVITE (g)

It is a measure of man's community that so many European tribes agreed at an early stage that spirits were – as acquavite translates – "the water of life." Acquavite is an Italian general term for spirits. The more common Akvavit and Aquavit spellings belong to Scandinavia. The French follow suit by calling their brandies collectively eaux-de-vie, and the idea recurs in the Gaelic *uisge beatha*, etymologically the parent of whisk(e)y.

ADVOCAAT (g) 15%

Dutch egg-and-brandy liqueur. Legend has it to be a misunderstood version of an equally thick avocado drink encountered by Dutch mariners in the West Indies. Others submit that it leads the drinker to talk with the eloquence of an advocate, or that it was once favored as a tipple by lawyers. In truth, it is a talkative drink only in that it is popular with gossipy old ladies in search of an innocent and sustaining pick-me-up, with teenage girls in a lemonade concoction called a *snowball*, and at Dutch christenings, for which occasion it may be flavored with cinnamon. Flavors such as mocha and chocolate are available in Germany.

AGUARDIENTE (g)

Fire-water? Well, perhaps "burned water." Generic term in the Spanish language for spirit drinks. In Spain it may specifically refer to a coarse brandy-like spirit made from grapeskins, stalks and pips, and comparable with French marc, Italian grappa, etc. In Latin America, especially Ecuador and Colombia, it can refer to a coarse sugar-cane spirit often flavored with aniseed.

AKVAVIT (g) 40–45%

Name broadly applied to all the principal indigenous spirits of the Scandinavian countries, irrespective of the flavor (also Akvaviittee and Aquavit). The akvavit spelling is most common in Denmark, where Aalborg is the most popular brand. A neutral spirit is produced from potatoes if they are in season, or from grain, and redistilled with flavorings, in the manner of gin. Caraway is the most popular flavor, although dill is also typical. Drink ice-cold in a small glass that has first been frosted in the refrigerator. An interesting aperitif with a chaser of beer and a marinated herring hors d'oeuvre. See also **Acquavite**.

ALE (g) ●

(Strengths vary widely.) The name in the English-speaking world (and also borrowed in Belgium, France, and Quebec) for a beer made with a top-fermenting yeast, which should render it fruity and complex in flavor. The majority of beers are (bottom-fermenting) lagers.

ALIZIERGEIST (g) 45%

Fruit brandy in the eau-de-vie style, made in Alsace from the berries of the wild service tree.

ALLASCH (g) 35–40%

Sickly speciality liqueur which is a version of **Kümmel** with the addition of almonds, aniseed, and other flavorings. Named after a castle in Latvia where the original was produced.

ALMOND

Several companies produce crème d'amandes (g), which is usually rather sweet. Crème de noyau (g) has an almond flavor, although it is commonly made from peach and apricot kernels. Crushed almonds are used in the production of **Amaretto** (g) along with apricots. Non-alcoholic almond syrups such as **Orgeat** are also used in cocktails.

ALT

The German word for old, specifically applied to the top-fermented, copper-colored beers of North Rhine-Westphalia, notably produced in Düsseldorf and Munster. "Old" because top fermentation predates the bottom-fermentation method used to produce the better-known German beers. Altbier (g) 4%+ is served in cylindrical glasses. It is also the basis of a springtime fruit punch.

AMARETTO (g) 24–28% ●

After-dinner liqueur with almond flavor, made in Italy from apricot kernels, and very popular in the United States. Said to have first been made in Saronno in 1525 as a tribute to artist Bernadino Luini by his model. The loving associations are underlined by a well-known brand called Amaretto di Amore (p). Sometimes served super-indulgently with delicious amaretto-flavored biscuits wrapped in tissue paper. Useful in the cocktail bar, and occasionally in the kitchen.

AMARO (g)

The Italian word for bitter. Generically used to describe the many patent bitter liqueurs produced in Italy. Amaros, usually dark brown in color, are made from herbs, plants, and tree barks. They are diluted and served with ice as aperitifs, and served neat as digestifs. There are at least 500 established brands, some containing little alcohol, others up to 45%.

AMARETTO HEARTWARMER *SOUTHERN COMFORT, DRY VERMOUTH AND AMARETTO COMBINE TO MAKE THIS ALMOND COCKTAIL.* *SEE PAGE 137.*

AMER PICON (p) 21%

Sometimes known simply as Picon (*amer* is French for bitter). Patent aperitif with a flavor of oranges and gentian. Evocatively French. On its own, syrupy and heavy, but wonderfully refreshing when served with a spot of grenadine, a little soda, several large ice cubes, and a slice of orange.

AMONTILLADO (g) 15.5–18% •

Second among the principal classifications of **Sherry**. An amontillado is darker than a **Fino**, and should have a dry but powerful and often nutty flavor. Serve with soup courses, or as a hospitable greeting, or chilled as an aperitif.

AMOROSO (g) 18–24%

A rich, sweetened version of **Oloroso** sherry. Serve at room temperature to sweet-toothed guests, as an afternoon drink, with fruit-cake or desserts, or after dinner.

AÑEJO

The Spanish word for old, applied in Hispanic countries to spirits (eg. tequila or rum) that have been aged.

ANESONE (g) 45%

An Italian aniseed and licorice-flavored drink similar to French **Absinthe** substitutes and Greek **Ouzo**.

ANGOSTURA (p) 45% •

The most famous patent bitters. Originally made in the town of Angostura, Venezuela, and now produced in Trinidad. Formulated by a military doctor in the Caribbean, with gentian as its most pronounced ingredient. Many cocktail and culinary uses, and as the "pink" for gin.

ANIS (g)

Term broadly used to cover all aniseed-flavored drinks, but more specifically referring to liqueurs with varying degrees of sweetness. In Spain, where the local **Absinthe** replacement is known as ojen (g) the term anis specifically means a liqueur of the syrupy type. These liqueurs, very popular in Spain, are available in both sweet and dry forms.

ANISETTE (g) 25–30%

French name for a sweet, aniseed-flavored liqueur. The most famous producer is Marie Brizard.

APERITIF (g)

A broad and a narrow meaning. Broadly, any alcoholic drink which may be taken before a meal to sharpen the appetite: well-hopped ales, dry champagne, dry sherries, most of the classic cocktails, and dry vermouths. More specifically, the term aperitif is used to describe patent drinks that are made especially for this purpose. Most, but not all, of these are pink or dark red. Their alcoholic content is usually around 20%. Some are a development of the vermouth idea. These include **Byrrh**, **Dubonnet**, **Lillet**, and **St. Raphaël**, all from France, and **Punt e Mes**, from Italy. Others are a gentle form of bitters, including **Amer Picon** from France, and **Campari** from Italy.

APOLLINARIS (p)

What **Perrier** is to France, Apollinaris is to Germany. It is the country's best-known mineral water, and its red-triangle trademark (similar to that of Bass beer) enjoys widespread recognition. It is naturally carbonated, but much less so than Perrier. It has a high mineral content, and its alkaline composition makes it an excellent soother of hangovers. The source is at Bad Neuenahr, in a wine-producing area downstream from Koblenz.

APPLE BRANDY see **Applejack** and **Calvados**

APPLEJACK (g) 45–50% ●

American name for apple brandy, once popular on the East Coast of the United States but now an esoteric speciality. On the West Coast, new producers use French terms such as *eau-de-vie de pomme* for clear or oak-aged versions. See also **Calvados**.

APRICOT BRANDY (g)

In many countries, products labelled as apricot brandy are made by the infusion of the fruit in a spirit base. Although this type of product is perfectly reputable, and is offered by most of the major distillers in Europe, it is not a brandy; it is a liqueur, usually with an alcohol content in the 20–35% range. In the United States, the government has created a category known as the flavored brandy. While some of the European products are based on neutral alcohol, and others on grape brandy, only the latter is permitted in this American category, and alcohol content must be a minimum of 35%. A true apricot brandy is not based on anything; it is distilled from the fruit. The most famous example is Barack Pálinka (p) 40%, which originates from Hungary and is made by the firm of Zwack in Vienna. Hungary still produces a fine Kecskemét apricot brandy. Similar confusion over production methods exists in the case of other fruit brandies, but to a lesser extent because of special generic terms which often identify the distilled product. Apples are distilled into **Applejack** or **Calvados**, cherries into **Kirsch**, plums into **Quetsch**, **Mirabelle**, or **Slivovitz**.

APRICOT LIQUEURS see above and **Abricotine** and **Apry**

APRY (p) 30–35%

An apricot liqueur of excellent quality made by the French liqueur house Marie Brizard.

PARK LANE SPECIAL (RIGHT) *MAKES EXCELLENT USE OF APRICOT BRANDY, GIN AND FRESH ORANGE.* **PEPPERMINT PARK** *MIXES CHAMPAGNE AND GIN.* *SEE PAGE 200.*

AQUAVIT (g) 35–50%

Although the best-known brand worldwide is Danish (see **Akvavit**), both Sweden and Norway produce spirits of this type. Norway's most famous brand, Linie (p), derives its name from an extraordinary tradition. The name means line, and refers to the equator. Norwegian seafaring tradition demands that the best aquavit should spend some time at sea before being drunk, and Linie crosses the equator twice on a journey to and from Australia before being put on sale. Each bottle is marked with the name of the ship on which it travelled, and the date of the voyage. The motion of the ship, the changes in temperature during the voyage, and the salt breezes are supposed to contribute to the characteristic softness of Linie Aquavit. Although Swedish aquavit is the least known internationally, it enjoys the largest home market. The state monopoly produces about 20 varieties, including the caraway type, which the rest of the world most readily recognizes as aquavit, but the bestseller locally is an unflavored brand. Although the Swedes use the term aquavit, they more commonly refer to hard liquor as *brännvin*. See **Swedish punsch**.

ARAK, ARRAK, ARRACK (g)

A word, of Arabic origin, describing any distilled spirit. An arak may be any Eastern spirit, from an aniseed- or licorice-flavored liquor in the style of **Raki** (a related word) to a pungent rum. It may be distilled from grapes, grain, dates, or coconut palm sap. The most famous, Batavia Arrak, is made in Java, Indonesia, from malted rice and molasses, and is aged for between seven and ten years. See **Swedish punsch**.

ARMAGNAC (g) 40% ●

The world's second great brandy, which the French have managed to keep largely to themselves. Although both cognac and armagnac come from the southwest of France, their centers of production are about 150 miles apart. The cognac-producing area lies well to the north of the town of Bordeaux, and reaches out to the coast; the armagnac country lies well to the south of Bordeaux and reaches out towards the Pyrenees. It is an area flavored by those mountains, and by the influences of Basque and Gascon history, and its famous brandy is produced in the *départements* of Gers and the Landes. While the countryside of Cognac is gentle, that of Armagnac is hilly and hot, Cognac has chalky soil, Armagnac has sandy soil; the cognac grape is usually the St.-Emilion (the local name for the Ugni Blanc), the armagnac grape, the Folle Blanche. While cognac is double-distilled in **Pot stills**, armagnac is single-distilled in its own hybrid variety of still – to a lower alcoholic content, and therefore retains greater flavor – before being aged and blended. Cognac is aged in Limousin or Tronçais oak while armagnac benefits from the dark, sappy, tannic Monlezun oak. At its best, cognac has sophistication and finesse; armagnac is rich and pungent. Cognac is universally recognized as the most elegant of all spirits, but armagnac is prized and in some cases preferred by connoisseurs. It is said, rather fancifully, to have been the brandy of d'Artagnan, and it is certainly mentioned in French history 200 years before cognac. Yet for many years most armagnacs went north to be blended into cognac, in which their color and character created an illusion of greater age. Today, armagnac age is indicated by the same labelling practices as in Cognac. The best quality come from Bas-Armagnac and Ténarèze, although the biggest of the producing zones is Haut-Armagnac. While cognac is dominated in the world market by big names, the production and marketing of armagnac is for the moment much more fragmented.

ASBACH (P) 40%

The best known of the German brandies, produced on the Rhine at Rüdesheim. Like cognac, the good-quality German brandies are aged in wood, usually Limousin oak. Well-known producers include Dujardin and Scharlachberg. A brandy conforming to the highest national standards in Germany is labelled as a *weinbrand* in the local market. A lesser confection may be called only a *branntwein aus wein*.

ASTI

Important Italian wine-growing region to the east of Turin, in the province of Piedmont. Famous for Asti spumante, a sweet and fruity sparkling wine, of low alcohol content, made from Moscato grapes.

AURUM (P) 40%

An unusual golden-colored liqueur of herbs and fruit with a sharp tang of orange peel, based on brandy. Produced at Pescara, Italy. The Aurum distillery company also produces other liqueurs.

B AND B (P) 43%

"Benedictine and Brandy" liqueur. Although Benedictine itself is based on cognac, it is sometimes taken with brandy; a slug of hard liquor knocks the sweetness off many a liqueur, while retaining the distinctive flavor. A "B and B" is said to have been a popular order in North America long before the Benedictine company put both drinks into one bottle, in 1938. By doing so, they ensured that their precious liqueur was not sullied with inferior brandies, and they made the profit on the cognac.

BACARDI (P)

Old, established firm of rum producers who moved from Cuba to Puerto Rico, and now have distilleries in several other places. Bacardi did much to popularize light-bodied rums during the 1960s. The name Bacardi was commonly used to describe a cocktail, a grenadine version of the Daiquiri, until the firm took legal steps to protect its trademark.

BAILEY'S IRISH CREAM (P) 15%+

A distinctive chocolate-flavored whiskey and heavy cream liqueur of low alcohol content produced in the Republic of Ireland. Formulated in the 1970s and one of the few totally new drinks to have enjoyed considerable success. Many imitators.

BACARDI SPECIAL *THE RUM, OF COURSE, MUST BE BACARDI. GRENADINE GIVES THE COLOR TO THIS OLD FAVORITE.* *SEE PAGE 141.*

BANANA LIQUEURS (g) 25–30%

Crème de banane is made in many countries. Bananas are macerated in neutral spirit, or artificial flavorings are used. An excellent banana liqueur is made in the Canary Islands from local fruit. The bottle is shaped like a bunch of bananas.

BARACK PÁLINKA see **Apricot brandy**

BARBADOS RUMS (g) 40%+

Good-quality, medium-light rums with a distinctively smoky flavor, made by both pot and continuous stills. Some very well-aged. See **Rum**.

BEERENBURG (g) approx. 30%

The national drink of Friesland, according to the Dutch. Although the long-lost European nation of Friesland is now largely shared between the Netherlands and Germany, it clings to its own traditions. Beerenburg was named after an Amsterdam herb and spice merchant but it was, and still is, the distinctive bitters of the Dutch province of Friesland. It is made from 15 herbs, including violet roots, angelica roots, gentian, and bay leaves, and its alcohol content varies depending upon the producer. In that part of Friesland which is in Germany, the "national" drink is **Friesengeist**, a unique mint-flavored spirit.

BENEDICTINE (p) 43% ●

Sometimes described as the world's oldest liqueur, because it was formulated in 1510. The particular Benedictines who devised this elixir had an abbey in the little seaside town of Fécamp, in the Caux district of Normandy. The abbey was sacked during the French Revolution, but in 1863 the formula for the liqueur providentially came into the hands of a local merchant, Alexandre le Grand, who is said to have been a descendant of a trustee of the abbey. After tireless effort and experiment, he finally managed to produce the liqueur with such commercial success that he was able to build a "palace" and art museum which is today a great tourist attraction. "To God Most Good, Most Great" says the Benedictine dedication Deo Optimo Maximo, which is initialled on every bottle. Twenty-seven of God's herbs, plants, and peels go into Benedictine, and some of them blossom on the cliffs nearby. The extraction by steeping and maceration, of essences and flavors, is a matter for great attention: the processes are many and complicated; a certain sequence must be followed; and production takes three years, followed by four years of aging. Benedictine is typical of drinks made by secret formulas. Innumerable imitators have failed to copy it convincingly, and the Germans have a whole genus of "Diktiner." It is for its individuality of character as much as its antiquity that Benedictine has become one of the world's most famous liqueurs. If any other enjoys a comparable reputation, then that must be **Chartreuse**.

BIANCO

Italian word for white. Often used as a generic term for the white variety of sweet Italian vermouth (16%), which has a tinge of vanilla in its taste. Although both bianco and rosso (red) are sweet, the latter is slightly less so, due to the influence of *Absinthe gentilia*. Dry white vermouth is identified simply as secco.

BITTER (g) 3.5–5.5%

The principal type of ale consumed in England and Wales, most often on draught. The term refers to the bitterness provided by hops. Traditionally, most brewers also made a less hoppy draught ale, described as Mild.

BITTER STOUT see **Dry stout**

BITTERS (g)

Wide-ranging term for bitter essences and alcoholic drinks made from roots, flowers, fruits, and peels macerated in neutral spirit. Common ingredients include orange, gentian, and quinine. Apart from orange and peach bitters for use in the cocktail bar, there are innumerable patent potions, in several quite different categories: the dash of bitters (35–45%), which may be **Angostura** (Trinidadian), Péychaud (Franco-American) or even hangover-curing Underberg (German); the bitter aperitif which fraternizes with the vermouths, typical examples being **Amer Picon** (21%) from France, and **Campari** (24%) from Italy; the versatile aperitif-or-digestif type of 40%+ which might also double as a hangover cure, like **Fernet Branca** from Italy and sometimes France or Jägermeister from Germany; and the contrarily sweet bitters of 30%+, such as the Italian **China-Martini** or the Spanish **Calisay**.

BLACKBERRY LIQUEURS approx. 30%

Made by the maceration of blackberries in spirit or brandy. Sometimes red wine or eau-de-vie is added to the mixture. The Polish Jerzynowka (p) is a good example. Silesia gave birth to a distinctive liqueur of wild blackberries called Kroatzbeere (p) in Germany. It avoids the sickly sweetness of many liqueurs, has an excellent bouquet, and an alcohol content of 30%.

BLACKCURRANT •

Several blackcurrant liqueurs are made in different parts of the world, but the most famous come from France from the Dijon area where they are known as crème de **Cassis** (g). These Burgundian cassis liqueurs (15%+) are made by the maceration of blackcurrants in neutral spirit or eau-de-vie. Small quantities of other berry fruits and sugar may be added. Burgundian cassis is widely used as a mixer, with chilled white wine, champagne and vermouth, to produce a typically French aperitif, or with cognac to create a rich after-dinner drink. Blackcurrants are also distilled into a true brandy of about 45%, known as *eau-de-vie de cassis*.

BLENDED WHISKY, WHISKEY

The biggest-selling Scotches on both sides of the Atlantic are blends, and this is likely to be true of any whisk(e)y that doesn't trouble to say otherwise. The Scots blend the cheaper but less flavorsome continuous still grain whiskies with the more expensive and distinctive **Pot still** malts to produce a compromise on both price and palate. In the U.S., a distiller may blend several straight whiskeys with a lesser whiskey, or with neutral spirit.

DUBONNET CASSIS *DECIDEDLY FRENCH, MARRYING THE BEST KNOWN OF FRANCE'S PATENT APERITIFS WITH BURGUNDIAN BLACKCURRANT LIQUEUR.* *SEE PAGE 165.*

BOCK (g)

German term for a strong beer. Especially associated with Munich, Bavaria, though famous examples are made in Kulmbach and the style almost certainly corrupts the last syllable of Einbeck, a town in Lower Saxony. *Bock* (various spellings) means billy goat in some Germanic languages, hence the frequent symbol on the label. Bock beers are especially consumed in cool weather, as a "warming" drink. "Single" Bocks usually have more than 6% alcohol and "doubles" around 7.5. In the U.S., Samuel Adams has a Triple Bock of 17.5.

BOLS (p)

Popularly associated with its old Hollands gin, which comes in a stoneware crock, Bols is an internationally known drinks company making a large range of typically Dutch products. In addition to that stonily proud "Z O Genever," Bols produces a number of other Dutch gins, old, young and flavored, under various brand names, and a large selection of liqueurs, many of which originated in the Netherlands. These include **Crème de Cacao**, **Curaçao**, **Parfait Amour**, and esoteric specialities such as Tip van Bootz and Hansje in de kelder. Lucas Bols, who went into business in Amsterdam in 1575, may have been the world's first commercial distiller. Among the several other important Dutch gin and liqueur firms, only De Kuyper has a substantial name outside the Netherlands, although there are many excellent small houses. See **Jenever**.

BOONEKAMP (p) 35%

A **Bitters** which lives up to that description with a dry, daunting determination. Its forename is Petrus, and its surname is pronounced *bone-a-camp*. Its formula dates back to 1743 and is Dutch, but Boonekamp later became a German taste, and now enjoys a particular reputation among the bitter-bibbers of Italy.

BORDEAUX (g) see **Claret**

BOROVICKA (g) 35–40%

Eastern European spirit of the gin family, similar in style to German **Steinhäger**. See also **Gin**.

BOURBON (g) 40–50%+ •

It was from a river port in Bourbon County, Kentucky, that whiskey was famously shipped down the Ohio and Mississippi rivers to the fleshpots of New Orleans. Presbyterians from Scotland, via Northern Ireland, had made rye whiskey in Pennsylvania and Maryland before helping to open the state of Kentucky, which was better suited to "Indian corn." Distilling started in the late 1700s, and the industry is still concentrated in Kentucky.

The state stands on a limestone shelf, which gives up hard water (and calcium-rich "blue" grass to strengthen racehorses' bones). At least 51% of the whiskey mash must be corn, the rest being rye (for added flavor) and malted barley (for fermentability). Column stills are used, but the distillation is not sufficiently exhaustive to remove the sweet, creamy flavors of the spirit. Vanilla-like and fruity components come from the use of charred new oak in maturation. The wood of the barrels is very influential. The best are chosen for "Single Barrel" or "Small Batch" bottlings. "Kentucky Straight Bourbon Whiskey" must be at least four years old. See **Corn Whiskey**, **Rye**, **Sour Mash**, and **Tennessee Whiskey**.

BRANDY (g) 40–50% •

In several languages, the word for spirits derives from the word meaning to burn. The allusion is not to firewater, but the process of distillation itself. The first distillers were seen to apply fire to various liquids, apparently to burn them until they vanished in vapor before being reconstituted in a different form. In the languages of northern Europe, to brand is to burn. Brandy has come to mean a distillate, although not of grain but of fruit. Any fruit, having been fermented and then distilled, is a brandy. Any spirit distilled from fruit is a brandy. All the famous fruit distillates of Alsace and the neighboring parts of Germany and Switzerland, what the French call *eaux-de-vie* (and in so doing pick up another linguistic thread in the description of spirits), are all brandies, whether they are made from cherries into kirsch, from an endless assortment of berries, or from various plums. If a fermented mash of apples is distilled, that is a brandy, whether or not it is entitled by the place of its birth also to be a calvados. If grape skins are distilled into marc (or grappa, or tresterschnapps, or whatever), that is a brandy of sorts. Most conventionally, a wine distillate is a brandy, whether it be humble and homeless or a haughty armagnac or a fine Champagne Cognac. "Brandy" with no further qualification has therefore come to mean a grape distillate. What is not a brandy is a neutral spirit which has been flavored with fruit; that is a liqueur. See **Armagnac**, **Calvados**, **Cognac**, **Eau-de-vie**.

BRISTOL CREAM (p)

Brand name of an **Oloroso** sherry shipped by Harvey's, of Bristol, in England.

BROWN SHERRY (g)

Imprecise term used in British markets to indicate a particularly dark and sweet **Oloroso**.

BRUT (g)

A bone-dry champagne without the customary dosage of sugar-sweetened wine. This dosage varies between 1% and 10%, depending upon the type of champagne being made. After brut, in descending order of dryness, come extra sec or extra dry (in reality, just dry), sec (slightly sweet), demi-sec (sweet), and doux (very sweet).

BLACK VELVET *A VERY SIMPLE COMBINATION – CHAMPAGNE AND STOUT – YET THE RESULT IS HIGHLY SOPHISTICATED AND SENSUAL.* *SEE PAGE 144.*

BURGUNDY (g)

If Champagne is set aside as a special case, then France's two greatest wine regions are Bordeaux (see **Claret**) and Burgundy. Located in the center of eastern France, Burgundy was a kingdom in the Middle Ages, and politically it remains an important region. With Dijon as its main town, it is almost as famous for its gastronomy as for its rich, sonorous red wines. Burgundy popularly means red, but the region also has many fine white wines, including the great Chablis. Its winegrowing areas, and just a sampling of their famous districts, are: Beaujolais (Fleurie), Mâcon (Pouilly-Fuissé), Châlon (Montagny), Beaune (Montrachet), Côte de Nuits (Nuits-St.-Georges, Gevrey-Chambertin), and Chablis. The principal grapes of Burgundy are the Pinot Noir (red) and the Chardonnay (white). In the U.S., the term burgundy is sometimes used to describe an undifferentiated red wine.

BYRRH (p) 17%

French patent aperitif of the vermouth type, dryish and of medium weight, with a kiss of orange and quinine.

CACAO, CRÈME DE (g) 25–30% •

Chocolate liqueur produced in colorless and brown versions, the latter sometimes also flavored with vanilla. The word Chouao on the label means the cacao beans come from Venezuela, Chouao being a suburb of Caracas. Crème de cacao is useful in both the cocktail bar and the kitchen, and is a popular drink in the Marseilles area. It is sometimes drunk through a layer of cream.

CALISAY (p) 33%

The speciality of Catalonia, and a liqueur well-known throughout Spain. Made in Barcelona to a recipe which is said to have originated in Bohemia, Calisay is a slightly syrupy quinine liqueur. It is sometimes chilled as an aperitif, but works better as an after-dinner drink. Calisay is also used in desserts and cakes.

CALVADOS (g) 40–50%

One of the world's great brandies, the finest of apple distillates, and a proud speciality of Normandy with its own appellation contrôlée and réglementée regions. The finest calvados come from the appellation contrôlée region known as the Pays d'Auge and is double-distilled in a **Pot still** before being aged for at least one year. In practice it is usually matured for several years in oak casks. Good calvados is very dry and smooth, with a subtle bouquet. Not only is it drunk after meals but also as a refresher between courses by the delightfully gluttonous Normans. Lest their palates should momentarily forget the apple, they also use calvados extensively in their formidable cuisine. The *département* of Calvados is said to have taken its name from a galleon of the Spanish Armada which was wrecked on the Normandy coast as it fled from Sir Francis Drake. Apple brandy from outside the calvados appellation réglementée region may be called only *eau-de-vie de cidre de Normandie* (or Bretagne, or Maine, or wherever).

CAMPARI (p) 24% ●

Internationally, the best-known Italian patent aperitif. Commonly drunk on the rocks with soda, and the basis of two famous cocktails, the Americano and the Negroni. Campari is very dry, with a pronounced quinine taste. In Italy, visiting professors of Campari find it hard to avoid the rather weak pre-mixed soda version. Half the fun lies in getting the mix just right, and contemplating the rich, translucent red liquid as it refracts the midday sun.

CAMPBELTOWN MALT WHISKY (g) 40–45%+

This little town is on the Mull of Kintyre, a Scottish peninsula otherwise known for a song by Paul McCartney. It was an early center of whisky production, but now has only two distilleries, the underrated Glen Scotia and the justifiably renowned Springbank. Both make single malt whiskies in which the sea air of the peninsula can be detected on the nose. Springbank uses a system of three stills, but also has a heavier, double-distilled whisky called Longrow, made from a peatier malt. The grain is malted at the distillery. Campbeltown is also a center for the bottling of rare malt whiskies, by the respected firm of Cadenhead.

CANADIAN WHISKY

(g) usually 40% •

A crisp, spicy style of blended whisky. Small proportions of straight rye whisky, sometimes also a Canadian-made **Bourbon** type, and occasionally fruit juices, are blended with a less flavorsome grain whisky. The rye, or "bourbon," is made in a column still. In some cases, the grain whisky is also distilled from rye. In a blend, the youngest whisky may be four years old, the most mature up to 18.

CANE SPIRIT (g)

A white rum, distilled almost to neutrality, from South Africa.

CASSIS, CRÈME DE (g)

See **Blackcurrant**. A quite different Cassis is a lively white wine from Provence. The two can be mixed to advantage.

CHABLIS (g)

One of the world's greatest dry white wines, from Burgundy, although elsewhere in the world the name is applied to products which bear no resemblance to the original. A greeny-gold wine of which Hugh Johnson says in *The World Atlas of Wine*: "It is hard but not harsh, reminiscent of stones and minerals, but at the same time of green hay." In the U.S., the term is often used to mean an undifferentiated dry white wine.

KIR *A VERY PRETTY LITTLE COCKTAIL – PERFECT FOR PARTIES OR FOR AN EASILY PREPARED APERITIF. A DASH OF CASSIS WITH DRY WHITE WINE.* *SEE PAGE 188.*

CHAMPAGNE (g) •

In order to be worth drinking from a pretty girl's shoe, sparkling wine must not only have been grown within cork-popping distance of Rheims and Epernay but must also have been made by the champagne method. Champagne is a region nearly 100 miles northeast of Paris, around Rheims and Epernay, with outposts in the Aube *département*; the champagne method is a means of imparting the sparkle by secondary fermentation in the bottle, not in a large tank, and, perish the thought, not by artificial carbonation. If either of the first two methods is used, the sparkle will persist in the glass, but artificial carbonation produces only the most ephemeral spasm of excitement. A vintage champagne may take eight years or more to reach maturity. Showmanship aside, it should not pop noisily, but merely utter the sigh of a satisfied woman. A good champagne has a tantalizing combination of delicate beauty and racy promise. It should be thoroughly cooled, but not icy. Pinot and Chardonnay grapes are used. Good sparkling wines, *vins mousseux*, are made elsewhere in France, notably in Alsace, Burgundy, Limoux, the Loire, and Savoy.

CHAMPAGNE COGNAC (g)

Although the soil in the best Cognac region is similar to that in Champagne, there is no connection whatever between the sparkling wine and the brandy. *Champaigne* is the Old French word for an expanse of open country. The cognac-producing region is divided into six districts, among which the two producing the finest brandy are called Grande and Petite Champagne. In fact, the Cognac region is a quite different part of France from the home of champagne wine.

CHARTREUSE (P) 55% GREEN, 40% YELLOW •

Of the famous herbal liqueurs, this is the most sophisticated. Such rich and aromatic elixirs are perhaps an acquired after-dinner taste, but their inscrutability is quite provocative. The Carthusian brothers assure us that their basic *"élixir végétal"* and its derivative liqueurs, despite their memorable colors, contain not even the most innocent of dyes, but merely 130 herbs and spices which are variously infused, macerated, and distilled, and then aged for some years in enormous oak casks, watched over by monks. Chartreuse even continues to mature very slowly in the bottle. "Exceptionally well-aged" versions are sometimes produced. Chartreuse is the oldest among those liqueurs which are still produced by monks, and it has the obligatory romantic story. The formula dates back to the 16th century, but the process was not perfected until 1764, and commercial production did not begin until 1848. There were various alarums and excursions, and at one stage the monks were exiled to Spain, where they began a distillery which still operates in Tarragona. That establishment is visited once a year by the only three monks from France who know the formula. The main distillery is 15 miles from the monastery of Chartreuse, which itself is in wooded countryside in the foothills of the French Alps near Grenoble. Chartreuse is commercially marketed by a lay company. There are many liqueurs *vertes* and *jaunes* which affect a similar style, and the Germans have what they call "Kartäuser" digestifs.

CHÉRI-SUISSE (P) 30%

Swiss liqueur with the flavor of cherry-filled chocolates. To be placed gently between the cherry lips of a woman who needs a little indulgence.

CHERRY BRANDY (g) •

Term commonly applied with some imprecision to cherry liqueurs (see **Apricot Brandy**). Several styles. The Danes produce the type which has a dry tinge, a pleasing "almond" bitterness from the pit, as exemplified by Peter Heering (p), a brand which enjoys a considerable reputation. Several similar cherry liqueurs are produced in the Netherlands, among which De Kuyper (p) is one of the best known. Although the kernel is used in maraschino, this clear cherry liqueur, with intense flavor and flowery bouquet, is quite sweet. **Maraschino** (g) 30–40% is made from the marasca cherry of Dalmatia, and its bottle is typically encased in straw. Drioli first made maraschino in Zara when it was part of the Republic of Venice. When the area became a part of Yugoslavia, and although production of maraschino has continued in this region of the world, Drioli moved to the city of

Venice, and the famous firm of Luxardo to Padua. The cherries are now grown in the Po Valley. Further east, the Slavic countries also produce a cherry liqueur called Wisniak (g), approx. 25%, and an excellent cherry-flavored vodka, Wisniowka (g) of 40%. A great many countries have cherry liqueurs, sometimes several types, and the French produce an excellent pale, light version called guignolet (g), in addition to a kirsch-based version, and kirsch itself, which is a true brandy. See **Kirsch**, **Kirschwasser**.

SINGAPORE SLING *ALL THAT COLONIAL DECADENCE AND SPLENDOR EVOKED SIMPLY BY MIXING GIN, CHERRY BRANDY, LEMON JUICE AND SODA.* *SEE PAGE 209.*

CHIANTI (g)

One of the best Italian wines, and certainly the most widely known, though often through imitations. The Chianti area covers the better part of Tuscany, and the "Classico" wines come from the lovely hills between Florence and Sienna. A number of different grapes are used, but almost all Chianti is red. In its straw-wrapped flask, beloved of restaurant decorators and table-lamp makers, it has a refreshing prickle induced by adding a little unfermented dried-grape must. If it comes in a claret bottle, it is untreated Chianti, of the best, and has been aged in oak.

CHINA-MARTINI (p) 31%

The first word, pronounced rather like *keener*, is a reference to the quinine in the drink. Martini and Rossi, of vermouth fame, are the makers. Despite being 180 years old, this patent liqueur is little known outside Italy, although it can now be found elsewhere and is well worth trying. As an aperitif, it is diluted with two parts of slightly sweetened lemon juice, and perhaps a swoosh of soda, and served over ice. More commonly it is drunk as an after-dinner liqueur. China-Martini is a slightly syrupy drink, and is said to be the only "sweet bitters" in Italy. It is also made into a toddy with hot water and lemon juice.

CHOCOLATE

Rather sweet chocolate liqueurs, sometimes with additional flavorings of coffee, mint, nuts, or fruit, are made in various parts of the world. They are not to be drunk until after eight in the evening. The best known is Chocolat Suisse (p). This precocious confection even contains floating chocolate pieces. In Britain, a whole range of flavored Royal Chocolate (p) treats has been devised by liqueur expert Peter Hallgarten (member of a well-known wine-shipping family, and author of a much-respected study, *Spirits and Liqueurs*). See **Cacao, crème de**.

CINZANO (p)

One of the best-known **Vermouth** houses in Italy, the other being Martini and Rossi. Both are near Turin.

CLARET (g) •

A description bestowed by the English on the graceful red wines of Bordeaux. The use of the term claret probably derives from England's rule over that part of France in the Middle Ages. The word is imprecise in meaning, and carries no weight or authority, yet it has passed into the popular terminology of alcoholic drink. The wines of Bordeaux are the best known of all the wines that France produces, especially the reds. But only half the Bordeaux production is red, and a number of different grape varieties are used. Few of the famous districts of Bordeaux are wholly monochrome in any sense of the word. Although the Médoc is famous for red wines, Margaux also produces a little white; Pomerol and St.-Emilion are known for their reds; Graves is known for whites, but also produces red wines; Barsac and Sauternes are famous for their white wines; Entre-Deux-Mers produces mainly white. Among the famous châteaux of Bordeaux, Lafite, Latour, and Mouton-Rothschild are all in Pauillac. Hugh Johnson says in *The World Atlas of Wine*: "Many claret-lovers would tell you that the wines of Pauillac have the quintessential flavor they look for in Bordeaux – a combination of fresh soft fruit, oak, dryness, subtlety combined with substance, a touch of cigar-box, a suggestion of sweetness. Even the lesser growths of Pauillac approach their ideal claret."

COGNAC (g) 40% •

The most elegant of all brandies. To bear the appellation they must come from a delimited region around the little town of Cognac, including the basin of the River Charente, and the small islands off that coast, in the Bay of Biscay. The grapes have never made good wine, but they make the finest brandy, especially where the topsoil is chalkiest. The cognac-producing region is divided into six districts, of which the most chalky is Grande Champagne (nothing to do with the sparkling wine – see separate entry). Then, through Petite Champagne to the district called Borderies, the soil is less chalky, giving less finesse, but a fuller body and a higher flavor. Cognacs become less delicate, and progressively earthy, through Fins Bois, Bons Bois, and Bois Ordinaires.

All cognac must be distilled twice, in **Pot stills**, and aged for not less than two years, in oak. Most good cognacs are aged for at least three years, and usually far longer, and all are blended. A three-star label is not intended specifically to convey the age of the brandy; a three-star cognac is likely to be the firm's standard brand, its youngest and cheapest blend. A five-star label has precise meaning. No cognac of less than four and a half years may be used in a brand which is labelled VSOP (these initials stand for Very Special Old Pale, in English, and evidence the historical importance of trade with Albion). These cognacs are sometimes labelled reserve, or described as liqueur brandy. They are not liqueurs as understood by the English, but in the French sense of a fine after-dinner drink. A "Napoléon" brandy must be at least five years old, and this grandiose style has no more meaning than that, whatever else may be implied. Some firms produce a "Napoléon" and then a slightly older blend, with a shoulderful of epithets: *grande réserve, extra réserve, extra vieille, très vieille, cordon bleu, cordon argent, âge inconnu*. The last seems rather disingenuous, since brandy deteriorates after about 70 years in the cask. In the bottle, it does not age at all. See **Armagnac**, **Champagne cognac**, and **Eau-de-Vie**.

COINTREAU (P) 40%

Liqueur house best known for its **triple sec** (g). The latter description, implying something very dry, is a misnomer. *Triple sec* is a sweet clear liqueur with the flavor of **Curaçao** oranges.

CONTINUOUS STILL

A mixed blessing, since its talent for the light-bodied or even tasteless spirit, its efficiency and economy, and its ability to produce the same product irrespective of location or surroundings, place a terrible temptation before liquor producers and marketers. The continuous still in its various forms is also known as the column patent or Coffey still. It derives from the efficient continuous system of distillation pioneered in Scotland by Robert Stein and Aeneas Coffey in the late 1820s and early 1830s. Although Coffey was a former Inspector-General of Excise in Ireland his invention was not acceptable there, so he emigrated to Scotland. The Coffey still is used there today in the production of grain whisky, but the **Pot still** is used for malt whiskies, cognac, French fruit brandies, and most spirits of great character.

CORDIAL (g)

In the United States, a synonym for **Liqueur**. Although the word cordial may be more commonly applied to American products and liqueurs than to those from Europe, both in that context describe the same thing. The maker of a cordial/liqueur begins with a ready-made spirit base, in which he then infuses, macerates, or redistils flavoring agents. These may be roots, barks, flowers, fruits, or a mixture of several. The legal definition of a cordial or liqueur often says that it must be sweetened. Cordials and liqueurs are most commonly taken after dinner, and in many cases have a modest alcohol content. A redistillation of alcohol with herbs or fruit to produce a strong, dry drink is regarded as a flavored vodka or aquavit. In Britain, the term cordial is more often used for a fruit syrup with little or no alcohol.

CORENWIJN (g) 40%

A distinctive Dutch grain spirit of the highest quality, which might popularly be regarded as a type of schnapps. The base of corenwijn (corn wine) is rye, corn, and barley in equal amounts. It is triple distilled, and aged for several years in wood, retaining its own characteristic palate. Drink ice-cold, straight up, in a small Dutch gin or liqueur glass.

CORN WHISKEY (g) approx. 40%

An American rural whiskey containing not less than 80% corn, and aged in uncharred barrels. Although a bourbon is also made from corn, it may contain a lower percentage (minimum 51%), and it must be aged in charred barrels. See **Bourbon**, **Rye**, and **Tennessee whiskey**.

CREAM SHERRY (g)

A dark, smooth sweet **Oloroso**, sweetened with fortified grape juice.

CRÈME DE (g)

Liqueur in which one flavor predominates. Usually very sweet. Not necessarily implying that the liqueur contains or resembles cream.

CUARENTA Y TRES (P) 34%

Forty-three ingredients go into this brandy-based patent liqueur, which is very popular in its native Spain. Sweetish, with a vanilla taste on the palate.

CUBAN RUM (G) 40%+

Light-bodied rum used in the Daiquiri cocktail, which was named after a Cuban tin-mining town. Carta Blanca (P) is the main "white" brand and the golden Carta Oro (P) is colored with caramel. A light style of rum, made in continuous stills. A similar style is produced in Puerto Rico.

CURAÇAO (G) 25–40% ●

The eponymous island gave its name to a small, bitter, orange. As a Dutch colony it supplied these oranges to the liqueurists of the Netherlands. Some producers still use the term curaçao for an orange liqueur, which appears in various colors, from clear to blue. The colors are purely decorative, but very handy to the cocktail barman.

CUSENIER (P)

Well-regarded and long-established French liqueur house noted for its Freezomint (P) green crème de menthe.

CYNAR (P) 17%

Artichoke-based patent aperitif made in Italy, where it is well-known. Efficacious and excellent, unlikely though it may sound. Serve with two or three cubes of ice, and a swoosh of soda.

DOM see **Benedictine**

DANIEL'S, JACK (P) see **Jack Daniel's**

DANZIGER GOLDWASSER (g) 30–40%

The most spectacular of liqueurs in which glistening flecks of gold leaf float like a heaven-sent snowstorm. The gold is perfectly edible; indeed, it was originally added for its allegedly therapeutic properties. Goldwassers are flavored with caraway, aniseed, and sometimes orange peel. The original was made in Danzig (now Gdansk, Poland) by the firm of Der Lachs, currently based in Berlin. Goldwasser is one of the oldest liqueurs and has a brother called Silberwasser. Drinks of this type are popular among liqueur houses elsewhere in Europe and the Dutch also have a version called Bruidstranen (bride's tears).

DIGESTIF (g)

That the French should have a noun and the English language conventionally an adjective says much about the respective values of the two cultures. A digestif is an after-dinner drink. If it is not a sherry-aged single malt Scotch, a mellow brandy or a gentlemanly port, then it may well be a patent potion of mint, caraway, or Chinese rhubarb which would be an altogether less agreeable experience if taken in pharmaceutical form.

DORTMUNDER (g) 5%+

Style of German **Lager** beer which is slightly stronger and less bitter than **Pilsener** but drier than **Münchener**. Sometimes known in Germany as Export. Dortmund is Germany's biggest brewing city.

DRAMBUIE (p) 40%

The oldest and most famous whisky liqueur, romantically alleged to be produced from Bonnie Prince Charlie's own recipe, given to the present makers in return for their assistance to him. Drambuie, which means "the drink that satisfies" in Gaelic, is made from Highland malt whisky and heather honey. There are several other liqueurs based on Scotch, among which **Glayva**, made with herbs and spices, is the best known. Glen Mist is an excellent honey-flavored one, a little drier than its competitors. There is also an excellent Irish Mist from across the water.

DRY STOUT (g) 4.0–8.0%+

Guinness (p), from Dublin, is the classic example. Murphy's (p) and Beamish (p), both originally brewed in Cork, Ireland, are also excellent Dry stouts. Guinness and Murphy's are also brewed in a number of other countries and there are several such beers elsewhere in the world. Dry stouts have a far higher hopping rate, and a higher alcoholic content, than Sweet stouts, of which Mackeson (p) is the classic example. Other styles of stout include Oatmeal and Imperial.

DUBONNET (P) 17% •

Outside its home country, Dubonnet is the best known of the French patent aperitifs, with a deservedly high reputation. Although all the vermouth-style aperitifs are bitter-sweet, each has a different position in the taste spectrum; Dubonnet stands right in the middle. Its first taste is sweet, but it becomes smooth, with a tinge of quinine. The rich red kind is best known, but a blond version is popular in the United States.

EAU-DE-VIE (g)

"Water of life." The French generic term for all brandies. A grape brandy, whether haughty or humble, is an *eau-de-vie*, although it is not normally ordered as such in a French bar. If it is not ordered by its brand-name or region of origin, then it is identified simply as a *fine*, meaning the house *eau-de-vie de vin*. Since **Cognac** and **Armagnac** enjoy such pre-eminence in France, the lesser *eaux-de-vie de vin* often make themselves scarce, skipping overseas and calling themselves simply "French grape brandy." Among those that stay at home, the considerable authority the late Cyril Ray had a kind word for the grape brandy of the Champagne wine region, *fine de la Marne*. There are other interesting *fines*, and a variety of grapey oddities, all worth a try in the cause of experience. The term *eau-de-vie* also covers a brandy made from grape skins, *marc*, but that is really a different animal. The great apple brandy **Calvados** is an *eau-de-vie de cidre*, although this general term is in practice only applied to its less-esteemed brothers. In the absence of any qualification, *eau-de-vie* would most readily be taken to mean one of the superb fruit brandies for which Alsace is especially famous. These distinctive distillates are also known as *alcools blancs*, because they are colorless, having been aged not in wood but in glass or pottery. They are produced not only in Alsace but also across the borders in the Black Forest area of Germany and the north of Switzerland. Every available fruit is used, and among the best-known *eaux-de-vie* are those distilled from cherries (**Kirsch**), pears (**Poire William** in French, *birngeist* in German), Switzen plums (**Quetsch**, *zwetschenwasser*), **Mirabelle** plums, raspberries (**Framboise**, *Himbeergeist*), strawberries (**Fraise**, *Erdbeergeist*), and gentian (**Enzian**), the last very popular in Germany and Switzerland. These *eaux-de-vie* are distilled in **Pot stills** to an alcohol content of 38–45%, usually higher rather than lower. Schladerer is a large producer of excellent fruit brandies, but much of the business is in the hands of very small firms and home-distillers. Fruit *eaux-de-vie* are rather expensive, but they are eminently worth trying.

French Sherbert *Not as innocent as it sounds – a highly seductive combination of cognac, kirsch, champagne and water ice.* *See page 173.*

ECHTE

The German word for real. Sometimes used on labels of drinks to indicate "the real thing, from the original source." The word *urquell* is used with the same intention.

ENZIAN

The German word for gentian, the roots and flowers of which are extensively used in liqueurs. See **Eau-de-vie**.

ERDBEER

The German word for strawberry. Seen on the labels of liqueurs.

EVIAN

French spa town at foot of Mont Blanc which produces one of the best-known mineral waters.

FALERNUM (P)

A Caribbean syrup of mixed fruits containing very little alcohol, which is sometimes used to flavor and sweeten mixed drinks. Lime and ginger are pronounced ingredients. Confusingly, named after a famous wine of ancient times which survives in more modest form as the Falerno (both red and white) of modern Italy.

FERNET (P) 45% ●

A distinctive and very bitter herbal digestif made by Martini and Rossi, the vermouth specialists, in Turin. Its makers claim that theirs was the original of its type, and that rivals Branca, of Milan, followed them six months later. Such disputes are lost in the 1800s, when the mass-marketing of drink had its battle-scarred beginnings, but the Milanese Fernet-Branca is today the better known internationally. Both drinks are excellent, if acquired, tastes, but they are apt to be treated in some countries exclusively as hangover cures, in that they work on the principle of tasting so powerfully bitter that the victim can feel only better once he or she has swallowed them. See **Bitters**.

FINO (g) 17–18% ●

The finest category of **Sherry**. Pale, delicate, distinctive, dry. A wonderful aperitif.

FIOR D'ALPI (g) 40%

The twig in the bottle, gathering sugar crystals, adds a touch of color to these sweet liqueurs made from Alpine herbs. Mille Fiori is the same type of liqueur.

FORBIDDEN FRUIT (p) 32%

Tempting and tangy old-established American liqueur made from the shaddock grapefruit, with orange and honey, and based on brandy. Splendid spherical bottle.

FRAISE

The French word for strawberry. Usually denotes a strawberry brandy (see **Eau-de-vie**), but also to be found on the labels of liqueurs and even a flavored **Vermouth**.

FRAMBOISE

The French word for raspberry, seen on the labels of **Eau-de-vie** and **Crème de** framboise.

"FRENCH"

Once a popular term in England, and sometimes still used, for a dry **Vermouth**. To request simply a "gin and French" was to invite a measure of dry vermouth with the liquor. Originally, French vermouths were dry and Italian ones sweet, but the two countries have long produced both styles.

FRIESENGEIST (P) 45%

From the Frisian part of Germany, a powerful mint liqueur made by a small private firm. Frisian coffee is made not with milk from the region's famous cows but with this mighty mint, flambéed.

FUNDADOR (P) 40%

Outside Spain, probably the best-known Spanish brandy, and widely drunk in its home country. A good-quality label from the respected house of Domecq.

GALLIANO (P) 40% •

Mister H. Wallbanger made it famous in the United States by his curious deeds, but this swaggering liqueur from Lombardy has long been known in Europe, and is itself named after a famous man, an Italian war hero from the conflict with the Abyssinians in the 1890s. Major Giuseppe Galliano held out for 44 days at Fort Enda, which is depicted on the label, before being forced to surrender. In his memory was named this sweetish liqueur, golden in color, flowery, spicy, herbal, with a tinge of vanilla. Galliano is used increasingly in mixed drinks and its proud, tall bottle stands well on the cocktail bar.

GARNIER (P)

Famous liqueur house in France, well-known for its apricot liqueur.

GENEVER (g) see **Jenever**, also **Gin**

GIN (g) 37.5–47.3% •

The lower-strength gins are a new and regrettable development in Britain, home country of the London Dry and Plymouth types. Some British producers have commendably held firm against this kind of cheapening of the product. The English originally adapted gin from the Dutch **Jenever** or *genever* (or, occasionally, *geneva*). All of these names derive from juniper, known as *ginepro* in Tuscany, Italy, where the berries are harvested.

Gin is said to have been popularized by a Dutch physician, Franciscus or Sylvius Böe in Leiden in the 1500s, but may have first been produced in Belgium or the north of France.

Many flavorings have been used in drinks, but the defining element in gin, of whatever type, is the juniper. The best gins are made by the redistillation of a grain spirit though a bed (or muslin bag) of juniper berries. Others are flavored after distillation. The English style of gin uses a neutral spirit, and the junipers may be accompanied by coriander seeds, angelica, orris (iris root), cassia (the outer bark of the cinnamon tree), lemon or orange peels, almonds, and other botanicals. The European *jenever* type often has more of a grain character (typically barley malt and rye), but may also use coriander and perhaps caraway and aniseed.

GLAYVA (P) approx. 40%

A Scottish, whisky-based, liqueur flavored with honey and herbs.

GLENFIDDICH (P) 40%

Internationally the biggest-selling single malt whisky (the label, curiously, uses the term "straight"). This easily drinkable, lightly fruity, sweetish whisky is made by the family firm of William Grant at its distillery in the Glen (small valley) of the River Fiddich (pronounced with a guttural-to-hard "*ch*") at Dufftown. The Fiddich flows into the River Spey, the valley and tributaries of which are the most famous for Highland whisky. See **Highland malt whisky**, **Single malt**, and **Scotch**.

GLENLIVET (g)

The valley of the small River Livet (also in the Speyside region) was the home of the finest whiskies when distilling was legalized in the Highlands of Scotland in 1824. Only the valley's original distillery is

---

ORANGE BLOSSOM *A MORE SOPHISTICATED VERSION OF A GIN AND ORANGE-BASED COCKTAIL ORIGINALLY DEVISED TO DISGUISE PROHIBITION HOOCH.* *SEE PAGE 199.*

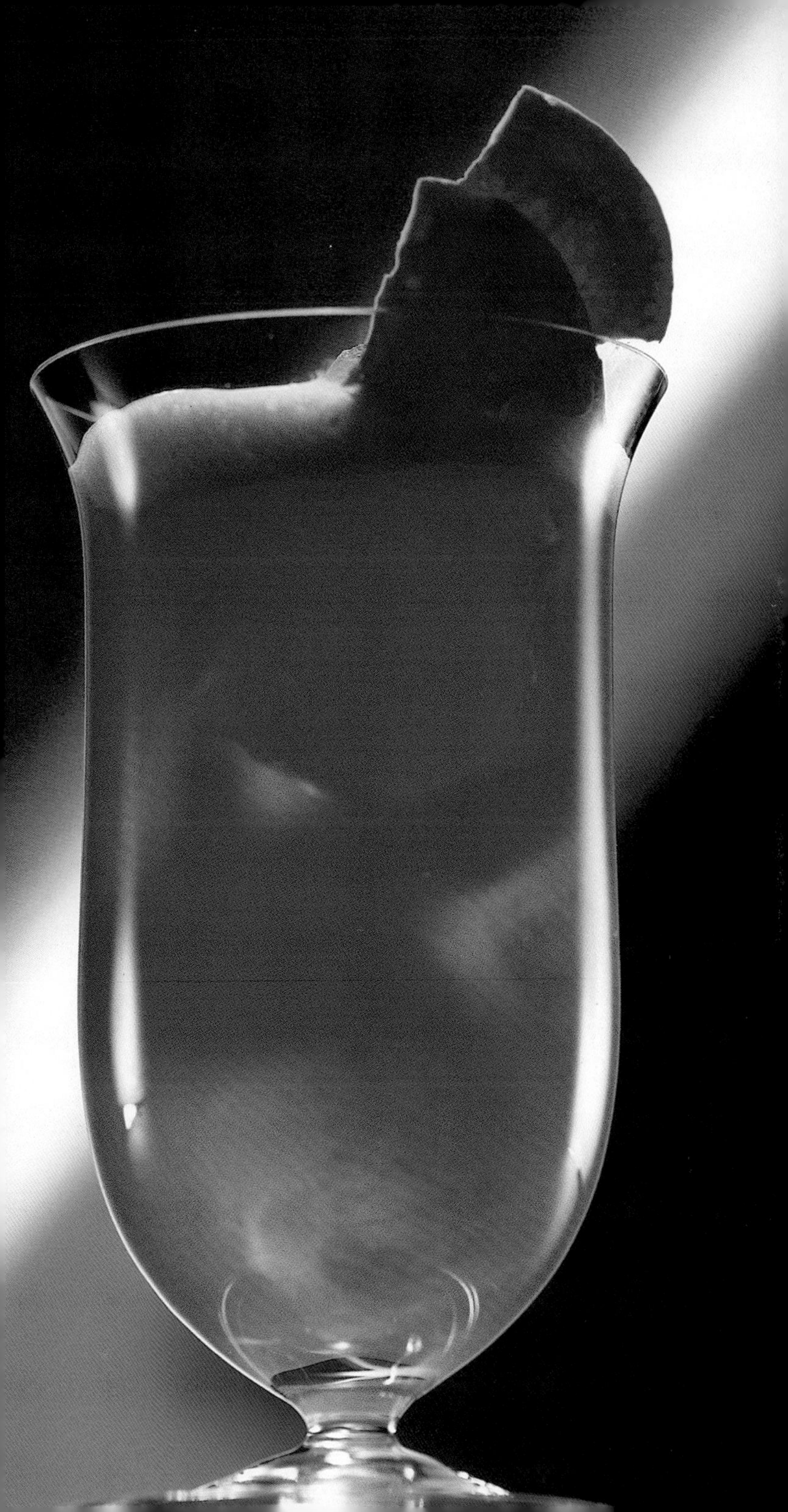

allowed by law to call itself *The* Glenlivet (p) (its still-renowned whisky is the biggest-selling malt in the United States). There are two other distilleries in the valley, Braes of Glenlivet and Tamnavulin, and a third, Tomintoul, in the parish. All of these distilleries produce light, flowery, elegant, single malt whiskies. Such is the fame of the glen that its name has been appropriated by (often well-respected) distilleries in other valleys, but this practice is gradually diminishing. See **Highland malt whisky**, **Single malt**, and **Scotch**.

GOLDEN RUM (g) 40%

Term commonly applied to rum of that color from Cuba, Puerto Rico and the Virgin Islands. Golden rum has a more pronounced taste and more character than its "white" brother, though both are of the light-bodied type. The color derives from caramel, and the rum is aged for a minimum of three years.

GOLDWASSER (g) see **Danziger Goldwasser**

GRAIN WHISKY, WHISKEY (g)

In Scotland, a continuous-still product made from unspecified grains (corn, wheat, or unmalted barley), and used for the purpose of blending (see **Blended whisky**). Scottish grain whisky is not distilled to the point of neutrality, and is aged for four years. The flavors can be tasted in the one or two single grain whiskies that are bottled. Though most American whiskey is produced from corn, the distillers also use this grain to produce neutral spirit for the purpose of blending. Some of this is aged and bottled as grain whiskey.

GRAND MARNIER (p) 35–40% •

A cognac-based orange liqueur of the highest quality, made by a respected French liqueur house. The fruit is of the **Curaçao** type, and it is steeped in the brandy. The yellow riband version is of a lower strength.

GRAPPA (g) 40%+

A coarse, country spirit that features in Hemingway novels. Grappa is the name used in Italy and California for a brandy distilled from the skins, pips and stalks of grapes, sometimes known as the pomace. Some grappa is distilled in a **Pot still**, some by a method in which steam is forced through the pomace in vessels rather like pressure cookers. Young grappa is very fiery, but it mellows a little with age and is sometimes matured in wood. Its character is very dry and woody, and inspires both a devoted following and a great deal of scorn. A sometimes finer version is made in France where it is called **Marc**. The same type of spirit is made in Spain as **Aguardiente**, in Portugal as bagaceira, in Germany as tresterschnapps, and under a variety of names in other countries throughout the world.

GRENADINE (g) ●

A sweet syrup flavored with pomegranate juice, containing little or no alcohol.

GUEUZE various spellings (g)

Highly unusual vinous wheat-beer traditionally brewed in the Bruegel country near Brussels. As in traditional winemaking, fermentation is promoted by such micro-organisms as are naturally present, without the addition of yeast as an ingredient. A gueuze beer is produced to various palates and strengths by the blending and aging of several basic brews, which are known as **Lambic** (or Lambiek). Lambic, which probably takes its name from the town of Lembeek, is often used as the basis for fruit beers, notably **Kriek** (cherry) and Frambozen or **Framboise** (raspberry).

GYOKURO (g)

Not a form of martial arts but a tea used in Japanese liqueur.

HAITIAN RUM (g) 40%

Medium-bodied **Rum** of excellent quality, twice distilled in a **Pot still**. Made from cane juice rather than molasses.

HEERING, CHERRY or PETER (p) 25%

Respected label of dryish cherry liqueur produced in Copenhagen. See **Cherry brandy**.

HEFE

The German word for yeast. In labelling, it indicates a high-quality sedimented beer or a humble type of brandy made from lees, the yeasty fallout of wine production.

HIGHLAND MALT WHISKY (g) 40–60% ●

"The Highlands" evokes the romance, the mountains and the snow-melt that seeps through cracks in the rock and rises from springs to make Scotch whisky. In fact, three-quarters of the 100-odd Scotch whisky distilleries are north of the "Highland line" which runs from the town of Greenock to Dundee. The first tranche has in general whiskies with a malty dryness; those in the Glen Livet and the other rivers that flow into the Spey are often heathery and flowery, sometimes with a hint of peaty smokiness; the distilleries further north tend to produce firmer, spicier, styles. It is a question of geology (from what type of rock does the water rise?) and vegetation (does it flow over rooty peat, heather, clover, or ferns?). In the far north the distilleries are on the coast, and pick up some sea-air character. See also **Campbeltown**, **Islay**, and **Lowland malt whisky**.

HOCK (g) ●

Imprecise English term for the white wines of the Rhine, and pedantically those of the Rheingau region since the word is an Anglicized abbreviation of Hochheim, a wine-producing town near

Wiesbaden. Though Hochheim's wines are of a very high quality, the best-known vineyards of the Rheingau are further downriver at Johannisberg. The Rheingau produces superb wines from the German Riesling grape, flowery and spicy, with a delicate balance between acidity and sweetness, and growing richer with age. Traditionally, hock is served in a glass with a thick, knobbly, tinted stem. The other wine-producing regions of Germany are Rhine-Hesse, Rhineland Palatinate (Pfalz), Mosel-Saar-Ruhr, Middle Mosel, Ahr, Nahe, Baden, Württemberg, Franconia, Saxony, and Saale-Unstrut.

HOLLANDS

From the Dutchman's adjective to describe the products of his own country, this word passed into the English language as a description for gin when the juniper spirit arrived from the Netherlands. See **Jenever**.

INFUSION

In the production of liqueurs, the steeping of fruit in water in order to extract flavor.

IRISH MIST (P) 40%

Liqueur produced in the old distilling town of Tullamore, from **Irish whiskey** and heather honey. Said to be based on a recipe taken to continental Europe by Irish refugees fleeing from the Tudor armies of England.

IRISH WHISKEY (g) 40%+ •

That coffee confection may have done much to popularize the Hibernian spirit in a heathen world, but this has proven to be a mixed blessing, obscuring the true position of Irish as one of the world's great drinks. The Irish have the world's oldest distillery, and they were probably the first people to make whiskey. It seems likely that they knew how to distil from grain in early medieval times, and that Irish monks took the skill to Scotland – as missionaries, of course. Although the two countries' national spirits today are much more closely related to each other than to their American cousins, they nonetheless differ very substantially. The Irish use indirect heat, which does not influence the taste; although the Scots these days rarely kiln all their malt over peat, they usually burn this material for a period. Irish is unusual in that it uses a substantial proportion of unmalted barley, which imparts the characteristically oily aroma and flavor (linseed oil? The smell of saddlery?). The Irish favor triple distillation (which perhaps enhances the smoothness of the whiskey). For many years only **Pot stills** were used, but now column stills are also employed. The Irish have been moving away from their traditional medium-heavy style towards a lighter whiskey. It is to be hoped that they do not take this moderation to extremes. What the Irish in novels and movies order as "a ball of malt" has much to commend it to the palates of the growing numbers of drinkers who seek flavor, character, and authenticity.

For all its tradition, the Irish whiskey industry is very small. The most Irish-tasting whiskeys, Redbreast, Jameson, Powers, and Paddy, are all produced in a complex of stills at Midleton, just outside the city of Cork. The famous Bushmills distillery (licensed in 1608) in County Antrim makes exclusively malt whiskey, in something of an Irish-Scottish style. This is bottled as a single malt (with a green label), but also features in two malty blends, the de-luxe Black Bush and the regular Bushmills, both leavened with grain whiskey from Cork. Although the Coleraine distillery has now closed, bottlings have still been released on occasion. All of these distilleries are owned by Pernod-Ricard. In an attempt to add an independent voice, a group of entrepreneurs has, partially using the facilities of defunct distilleries, produced an Irish malt whiskey near Dundalk, matured it at Kilbeggan, County Westmeath, and given it the Derry name Tyrconnell.

ISLAND MALT WHISKY (g) 40–60%

Whiskies produced on the Scottish islands often pick up a brineyness, sometimes taken simply from the air and on other occasions also from the soil and peat over which the distilleries' water flows. Some devotees feel this constitutes a style, though (as always) there are many interpretations of it. On Orkney the whisky from Scapa is salty and that from Highland Park peatier. On Skye the Talisker whisky is almost peppery. Mull's Tobermory has far less seaweed than it once did. The Isle of Jura whisky has a touch of misty pine woods. The most famous island, **Islay**, has the most distinctive whiskies of all.

ISLAY MALT WHISKY (g) 40–60%

Pronounced *eye-la*. A beautiful island, thickly covered in peat, which produces whiskies so strongly flavored and so dry that they are said to have the iodine tang of seaweed. Held in awe by connoisseurs, usually hated by first-time drinkers, the whiskies of Islay are, in tiny quantities, an essential component of most good blended scotches. Ardbeg has the smell of bonfires; Lagavulin the dryness of Lapsang Souchong; Laphroaig the most typically seaweedy, iodine note; Port Ellen pepper; Bowmore a perfumed smokiness; Bruichladdich a hint of iron; Bunnahabhain a nuttiness that seems far too mild for Islay; Caol Ila an olive-like intensity.

IZARRA (P) 50% GREEN, 40% YELLOW

The liqueur of the Basque country, made on the French side of the frontier, flavored with plants from the Pyrenees, and based on armagnac. Izarra is the Basque word for star. Although the original is an old-established patent recipe, its makers now use the name as a brand on their range of liqueurs. A frappé made with Izarra itself in equal proportion to armagnac is known as a Green Beret Basque. With its bouquet of mimosa honey, the liqueur is also a most agreeable addition to desserts and jellies.

JACK DANIEL'S (P) 45%

The best known of the two Tennessee distilleries (the other being George Dickel's). The early stages of production in Tennessee are much the same as those in Kentucky, even down to the much-vaunted **Sour Mash** (in which residue from the previous distillations helps give continuity to the next). Where the critical difference occurs is in the slow leaching through 10 feet of charcoal. This is an early filtration, before maturation, as distinct from the normal, far lesser, procedure before bottling. The Tennessee distillers argue that it removes harsh flavors, leaving a "purer" whiskey to age. Others suggest that it actually adds a charcoal taste. This process was first practiced in Lynchburg, Tennessee, on what became the Jack Daniel's site, by a distiller from Tullahoma, home of George Dickel. The charcoal leaching defines Tennessee whiskey, and at Jack Daniel's it takes place in a slice of Americana. Jack Daniel's is America's oldest working distillery, dating back to 1866. The company has done much to preserve the contemporary appearance of its hometown, Lynchburg, which insists that its population remains at 361. The George Dickel distillery opened in 1870.

JAMAICA RUM (g) 40–75% •

In its traditional form, the most rich, buttery, full-bodied and pungent of the rums in the manner of the old British Caribbean. Jamaica rums are still often shipped to England for oak aging and blending in bonded warehouses at ports like London and Liverpool. Hence the expression London dock rum. The most traditional of Jamaica rums are double distilled in **Pot stills**, and their special character derives from the re-incorporation of residues from various stages of production. The residue from the distillation itself, known as dunder, is fermented and then reused to promote a natural fermentation. This is the most elaborate such process in the production of alcoholic drinks, but it is to some extent reminiscent of the sour mash in whisky production and of various techniques used in the brewing of especially characterful beers. Perhaps the rather old-fashioned English insult "dunderhead" was originally aimed at someone whose mind appeared to have been dulled by rummy excess. A heavy rum made by the dunder process is known in Jamaica as a Plummer type (g), and an even heavier one as a Wedderburn (g). See **Rum**.

DANNY'S SPECIAL *A DELICIOUS AND REFRESHING BOURBON-BASED COCKTAIL, WHICH INCLUDES COINTREAU, GRAND MARNIER AND LEMON JUICE.* *SEE PAGE 161.*

JENEVER (GENEVER, GENEVA, ETC.)

(g) 35–40% •

Gin, in its original and unabbreviated form (see **Gin** for derivation). Also sometimes known as Hollands, or as Schiedam, from the name of the traditional distilling town, near Rotterdam. Today, the biggest distillery is nearer to Amsterdam, and the style of gin commonly used throughout the world is London Dry. As the more recent distillers, the English quickly adopted the technology to make a highly purified base spirit, and this highlights the flowery dryness imparted by the botanical flavorings; the Dutch, as in earlier times, persist with a less "pure" spirit that retains some of the flavors of its grainy base. This is produced from equal parts of rye, barley, and corn by a double distillation process in a **Pot still**. The resultant "malt wine" is then blended, according to the palate required, with a neutral spirit that has been redistilled with the botanical flavorings characteristically used in gin. Juniper is by definition the dominant botanical flavoring in all types of gin, and coriander is among the ingredients used in both English and Dutch types, but in the Netherlands caraway and aniseed are also significant. Unlike English gin, the Dutch type is aged, but young (*jonge*) and old (*oude*) variations differ more in style than maturity. Young jenever, which is the more popular in the Netherlands, is very lightly flavored, and can have a disappointing lack of character, though this varies from brand to brand. **Bols** produces a very neutral young jenever under its own name, but its Claeryn label has a *jonge* with an interesting balance of juniper and "malt wine." Old jenevers have a pronounced "malt wine" taste. The initials ZO, from the Dutch words meaning very old, have no precise implication.

Since production of jenever predates the division of the Low Countries into two kingdoms, a spirit of the same type is also produced in Belgium. The center for distillation there is the town of Hasselt, in Belgian Limburg, though the city of Ghent is known for its partiality to jenever. In both countries, there are tiny private distillers whose products are well worth trying. There are also fruit-flavored jenevers. The Dutch and Belgians drink their jenever straight up, very cold, in small tulip-shaped glasses, as an aperitif or a hard liquor, and it is commonly held that continental gins are not suitable for use with mixers because of their very pronounced taste. This is a debatable proposition. Young jenevers are not strongly flavored, and it is arguable whether Dutch gins are as aromatic as they are said to be. Cocktails are made successfully with rye and bourbon, which have a considerably fuller flavor.

JEREZ

Too difficult for the English to pronounce with the proper lisp, so the Castilian "Hereth" is **Sherry** elsewhere. The town of Jerez is the capital of the sherry-producing country, which runs between Cadiz and Seville, in Andalusia, the most southerly region of Spain. The English may have developed a taste for stolen sherry during the sacking of Spanish ports in the sixteenth century. Later, merchants from the British Isles established themselves in Jerez, and English ports like London and Bristol found their way on to sherry labels.

KABÄNES (P) approx. 35%

The liqueur of Cologne, a patent semi-bitter recipe of excellent quality, available outside its homeland in cities with large German communities, like Chicago.

KAHLÚA (P) 26.5% ●

Coffee liqueur originating from Mexico and very popular in the United States. Taken as an after-dinner drink, used in desserts, and employed in many mixed drinks.

KIRSCH, KIRSCHWASSER (G) 45% ●

The most famous of the fruit brandies made in the area where France, Germany and Switzerland meet (see **Eau-de-vie**), this one made from cherries. Kirsch is the French-language name. *Wasser* is added in the German-language version to indicate spirit distilled from the fermented fruit. If the fruit is first macerated in alcohol which is then redistilled, the suffix becomes *geist.* The French distil at a sufficiently low point to retain the flavor of the fruit, while the Germans aim for a drier, stronger spirit. Kirschwasser, a strong, dry, cherry distillate, is especially renowned when made in the Black Forest. It is used deliciously to moisten the Schwarzwalder torte, the typical gâteau of the Forest.

KLARER (g)

Generic term in Germany for clear korn **Schnapps**, or **Steinhäger** gin.

KÖLSCH (g)

The German word meaning "from Cologne," especially applied to an unusual pale, brass-colored, top-fermented beer unique to the city and its environs and popular there as both an aperitif and a digestif. Very well suited to the latter role because of its alkaline composition. A common local snack is a glass of kölsch (4.5%) with "half a hen," which turns out to be a wedge of cheese, or "Cologne caviare," which is a type of blutwurst, (blood or black sausage).

KORN (g) approx. 35%

Clear grain spirit drunk in northern Germany, often with a beer chaser. Korn, which originates in the Harz Mountains, is usually distilled in a **Pot still**, and sometimes aged.

KRIEK (g) 5–7%

Cherry beer of excellent quality which is traditionally a summer drink in the Brussels area. See **Gueuze**.

KRUPNIK (g) 35–40%

A sometimes coarse honey vodka made in the Slavic countries.

KÜMMEL (g) 35–45% •

A peripatetic liqueur made with caraway, cumin seeds, fennel, orris, and other herbs. In the beginning, as now, kümmel was made by **Bols** in Amsterdam. It is said to have been developed by the pioneer distiller Lucas Bols in the late sixteenth century. The drink is then reported to have been enjoyed by Peter the Great in extraordinary circumstances. He was apparently working incognito as a laborer in the Netherlands, learning shipbuilding techniques with a view to starting a Russian navy. He took kümmel east, the story goes, and it subsequently reappeared as a rather sweeter liqueur some centuries later in a distillery at Allasch Castle, near Riga, Latvia, bearing the label of Mentzendorff. Political upheavals took that particular recipe variously to Germany and, by some homing instinct, to the Low Countries. Similar travails affected the house of Wolfschmidt, which elevated kümmel to a crystalline majesty and a strength of 60%. Even the dry Berlin-style kümmel is now made in Hamburg where the Gilka label is properly held in very high regard. Such has been the determination of liqueurists to safeguard their kümmel recipes wherever they were obliged to travel. Their journeys make light of those experienced by the men of **Maraschino**, the monks of **Chartreuse**, and the house of Zwack, to name but a few.

KVASS, QUASS (g)

Coarse Russian "beer" made from rye bread and, unaccountably, sometimes emulated by home-brewers in the United States. The technique is, though, worthy of a certain veneration, since it has its origins in the ancient East.

LAGER (g) •

From the German word to store. An omnibus term for any bottom-fermented beer, whether its style is derived from Pilsen (or even Budweis) in Bohemia, Munich in Bavaria, Vienna, Dortmund or Einbeck ("**Bock**"). An overwhelming majority of the world's beers are made by bottom-fermentation whether their labels say so or not. Beers made in this way should be stored for some weeks by the brewer so that they mature before being sold, hence the name. Bottom and top refer to the position of the yeast as it settles in the fermentation tank. The technique of bottom fermentation came into widespread use in the mid- and late 1800s after Pasteur had helped both brewers and winemakers to understand fully for the first time how yeasts performed. Bottom fermentation offered beers of more stability, consistency and sparkle than had previously been achieved with top-fermentation (the method still used to produce ale, porter, stout, most wheat beers, and many Belgian specialities). The older method, however, is held by connoisseurs to produce beers of more flavor and character. In this sense, there is an analogy with the pot and patent methods of distillation.

LAMBIC, LAMBIEK (g)

Vinous wheat-beer made near Brussels. Still and cider-like, an acquired taste, with a devoted following. Commonly used in blends. See **Gueuze**.

LEROUX (p)

The name of a major American liqueur company.

LIGHT RUM (g) 4% ●

Refers to lightness of body, rather than color. A light rum may be colorless ("white" or "silver"), or it may be aged for three years or more, in which case it will have more flavor, and then be colored with caramel ("amber" or "gold"). The lightness of body is achieved by distillation initially to a high alcoholic content, in continuous stills. Like most spirit, the rum is diluted to the required strength for marketing. Light-bodied rums are the style of the Spanish-speaking Caribbean, and especially Cuba, Puerto Rico, and the Virgin Islands.

LIGHT WHISKY, WHISKEY

Term most commonly used in the United States, and reflecting a fear of flavor. The lightness is in body rather than color, though the two are sometimes mistakenly perceived as being directly related. The body of a Scotch whisky can be diminished if it is blended from a high proportion of grain, or if notably light malts are used. American light whiskeys are the product of distillation to a higher alcoholic content than is normal, followed by a greater degree of dilution. By being more thoroughly distilled than a regular American whiskey, they lose body. They are aged in uncharred casks.

LILLET (p) 17%

Only the practiced will publicly try the trick of squeezing the zest of lemon and flaming the spray over the drink with a match, but even a virgin Lillet is an aperitif of elegance and individuality. This French patent vermouth is among the lighter and drier of its type, with an orangey tinge. The most common version has a full white-wine color, but there is also a sweeter red Lillet.

LINIE AQUAVIT see **Aquavit**

LIQUEUR (g)

To the French, any after-dinner drink, as in liqueur brandy. To the British, specifically a sweetish drink created from a ready-made spirit base into which such flavoring agents as roots, barks, flowers, fruits, or seeds are infused, macerated, or redistilled. The term liqueur is also used in the United States, though American counterparts are often referred to, confusingly, as **Cordials**. In Britain, a cordial is a flavored syrup with little or no alcoholic content.

LONDON DOCK RUM see **Jamaica rum**

LONDON DRY GIN 37.5–47.3% •

Having come from the Netherlands (see **Gin**), juniper elixir was made more or less in the Dutch way (see **Jenever**) for two centuries. When William of Orange came from the Netherlands to rule over England with his consort Mary, one of the regime's first acts was to ban the import of French brandies, and grant every citizen the right to distil, both measures helping farmers to find outlets for their grain. The flood of amateurish gin which ensued was still in full spate when the people of Britain had to be anesthetized through the change from a rural life to that of the world's first industrialized and urban nation. It was then that gin became synonymous with exploitation and misery, and perhaps that is why distillers seized the chance to produce a spirit of greater rectitude when the technology became available with the introduction of the patent still from the 1830s onwards. While the Dutch stuck to their full-bodied gins, retaining the flavor of the grain, the English used the patent still to produce a neutral spirit base. Perhaps that removed the need for heavy, sweet flavorings, giving rise to the dry gins which became popular in London in the 1870s. The base spirit for London Dry gin may be distilled from grain or from some other raw material such as molasses, but it will have been rectified to neutrality before being redistilled with the botanical flavorings in a **Pot still**. While juniper is the essential ingredient of all gins, and coriander is common to both Dutch and English, there are certain additional botanicals which are especially favored by the London distillers, though each label has its own particular formula. The most significant botanicals used in the various London recipes are angelica root, cassia and cinnamon bark, orange and lemon peel, and almonds.

London Dry established itself in good time for the Cocktail Age. Since whiskies and brandies have a much fuller body, and flavorless vodka was then unknown in the West, the neutral background of London Dry gin made it the most suitable base for cocktails. Furthermore, its botanical flavorings match or complement those used in vermouth and in many of the liqueurs that are used in cocktails. As distillers elsewhere took up dry gin, it became accepted that London indicated the style rather than the place of production. Among today's British-made London-style gins, Gordon's has a good juniper character but in Britain sells at 37.5%; Beefeater gives more emphasis to the aromatic angelica root; Bombay Sapphire adds peppery "grains of paradise;" and Tanqueray returns to juniper, at 47.3. In addition to London-style gins made under license elsewhere, Ireland has a citrusy Cork Dry gin and Minorca a slightly oily variation on the theme. See **Plymouth gin**, **Sloe gin**.

LOVAGE (P)

Herbal alcoholic cordial of low strength drunk as a digestif, added to brandy, port, or rum, or used as a hangover cure in the west of England.

APERITIF PERRIER *A VERY REFRESHING APERITIF, ALLEGEDLY PERFECT FOR SETTLING THE STOMACH. IDEAL FOR NERVE-RACKING FIRST DATES.* *SEE PAGE 140.*

LOWLAND MALT WHISKY (g) 40%+

Without the Highland peat and heather, or island seaweed and breezes, Lowland malt whiskies tend to emphasize the clean sweet taste of malt. Most of them are on the light side, a number of them thanks to triple distillation. There are only a handful of Lowland malt whisky distilleries, and some of those are in mothballs. The most typical, readily available, example of these is Auchentoshan.

MACERATION

The steeping of fruit in alcohol in the production of liqueurs. This process may take as long as a year.

MADEIRA (g) 15–20% ●

Fortified wine from the island of the same name, in the Atlantic off the coast of Morocco. In addition to being fortified with brandy, madeira is heated for four or five months at a temperature of 120°F or more. While the original wine of the island was acidic and unpleasant, this process produces a distinctive drink of great character, with a caramel tang. There are four types: sercial is drunk as an aperitif, and resembles a fuller fino sherry; verdelho has a tinge of honey and a smoky taste, and is drunk either as an aperitif or a digestif; bual is a dessert wine; the dark, fragrant, soft malmsey is a famous after-dinner drink and weapon of the seducer. Although the island of Madeira is historically linked with Portugal, its wines were once in every well-found English home (see also **Port**), and were also popular in the United States. They remain important in French cuisine, and are extremely popular in northern Europe.

MÁLAGA (g)

Fortified wine from the ancient town of Málaga, on the south coast of Spain. Made by a complicated process involving the use of grape musts and dried grapes. Dark, sweet, and once fashionable, but now rarely seen outside of Spain and Latin America.

MALMSEY see **Madeira**

MALT WHISKY, WHISKEY (g)

In Scotland, a whisky made in a **Pot still** exclusively from malted barley. In the United States, a whiskey made in a **Continuous still** or pot still from not less than 51% malted barley. See **Scotch**.

MALVASIA

The grape used to produce malmsey (see **Madeira**), and rich "brown" wines elsewhere in the world.

MANDARINE NAPOLÉON (P) 40%

Elegant proprietary liqueur. Napoléon is said to have wooed his favorite actress with a similar citrus potion, and Francophiles in Belgium took up the theme. Confusingly, the French language describes as a mandarine what English deems to be a tangerine, and it is from this fruit that the liqueur is made. In this instance, Andalusian fruits are macerated in aged cognac by the respected liqueurist Alfred Fourcroy.

MANZANILLA (g)

A most unusual once-removed **Sherry** of excellent quality but highly individualistic palate. Not from **Jerez**, but from nearby Sanlúcar de Barrameda. Manzanilla is so extraordinarily dry that some people find it almost bitter, and it has a notably delicate bouquet. These two characteristics are both said to be imparted by the salty sea air. An excellent aperitif.

MARASCHINO (g) 30%+ ●

Distinctive type of cherry liqueur originating from Dalmatia, though the most famous marques are now made in Italy. Extensively used in cocktails. See **Cherry brandy**.

MARC (g) 40–45%

The French name for grape skins, and for the brandy that is made from them, the counterpart to **Grappa**, tresterschnapps, and others. Marc is said to be much more delicate than its cousins, but it still inspires derision and devotion in equal proportions. Even outside France the marcs of Burgundy enjoy some reputation, and among them the late brandyman Cyril Ray drew attention to Meursault. He also noted the marcs of Champagne and Alsace, in the latter case especially the Gewurztraminer. A Burgundian cheese soaked in the spirit is known as *époisses confit au marc*. This is not to be confused with *tomme au marc de raisin*, which is merely coated with grape pulp and pips for strong teeth and stomachs.

MARIE BRIZARD (p)

Famous French liqueur house noted for its **Anisette** and its **Apricot brandy**. The lady who founded the firm in the 1700s is said to have been inspired by a recipe she received as a gift from a West Indian whom she successfully nursed through an illness.

MARSALA (g) 15–18%

Like so many fortified wines, marsala was created with the aid of the British. In this case, a Liverpool merchant settled in the Sicilian port of Marsala, and supplied Nelson's fleet with wine from there. The marsala process employs heated grape juice, and the end-product has a burnt-sugar palate. One fairly dry marsala nonetheless offers itself as an aperitif, while lovers of sweet, dark wines find the more typical treacly style quite delicious. A sort of marsala liqueur is made with egg yolk and other flavorings, and the wine is an ingredient of the classic Italian dessert zabaglione. A bar can exist without marsala; a kitchen cannot.

MARTINI AND ROSSI (p)

Famous **Vermouth** producers with headquarters near Turin. Despite its size and international organization, Martini and Rossi is still a family firm. Signor Rossi gave his name to an aperitif bitters made by

GOLDEN BRONX *ANOTHER PROHIBITION COCKTAIL – GIN, VERMOUTHS, ORANGE AND LEMON JUICE. AN EGG YOLK MAKES IT A "GOLDEN" BRONX.* *SEE PAGE 148.*

the firm, and Signor Martini to the famous range of vermouths. Although the dry one is often used to effect in the cocktail of the same name, this is coincidental. One account has the cocktail being invented by a bartender called Martini in New York, and French vermouth was originally used. See also recipe for **Dry Martini**, page 162.

MARTINIQUE RUM (g) 40%+

At its best, very much the **Rum** (or *rhum*) of the French Caribbean. Full-bodied and pungent, made from cane juice rather than molasses and distilled in a **Pot still**. In some cases the dunder process (see **Jamaica rum**) is used.

MASTIKA (various spellings) (g) 40%+

Brandy-based anis or licorice liqueur resinated with the gum of the mastic bush. Made in the Balkans, Greece, and Cyprus.

MÉDOC (g)

Not only the wine from that district of Bordeaux but also a liqueur, Cordial Médoc (p), 40%. A curious concoction of flavors and herbs on a base of local wine.

METAXA (p) 42%

Fully flavored and aromatic brandy from the firm of the same name, Greece's biggest distillers. The grapes are usually from Attica. Greek brandy is sometimes rather sweet and sticky. It may even be further sweetened so that it qualifies as a liqueur, though to what purpose is not quite clear. The best of Greek brandies are quite agreeable, especially after a feast of kleftiko or bastourma.

MENTHE, CRÈME DE (g) 25–30% ●

Sweet liqueur flavored with various types of mint. The green version looks more interesting, but the "white" is exactly the same. Crème de menthe frappé is a refreshing and palate-clearing digestif, and the liqueur is extensively used in cocktails. Among the highly regarded brands are Freezomint (p) and the oddly named Pippermint Get (p).

MEZCAL (g) 35–45%+

The machismo spirit of Mexico, for anyone who fancies tripping south of the border. The mezcal is a plant of the genus agave or maguey. There are those who think its distilled juice tastes like old zapatos, though it could more forcefully be argued that some of the brands exported from the town of **Tequila** are unduly refined. No, it's not made from cactus.

MILK SHERRY (g)

British term for a smooth, sweet **Sherry** based on an **Oloroso**. There is no precise meaning, nor any precise distinction between "milk" and "cream" sherries.

MILK STOUT (g)

British term for a Sweet stout, traditionally made with a proportion of milk sugars (lactose, a by-product of cheesemaking). The law in Britain no longer permits the term "milk" to be used on the label, although the designation still survives in Guernsey and Malta. See **Dry stout**.

MIRABELLE (g) 45%

Fine "white" brandy of the **Eau-de-vie** type distilled from the yellow Mirabelle plum in France, Germany, and Switzerland.

MISTELLE (g)

A mixture of surplus brandy and fresh grape juice of the same locality. The word mistelle may be used colloquially to describe this blend when it has been aged to produce a sweetish but substantial aperitif known as **Ratafia** (especially in the Champagne area) or **Pineau** (especially in the Charentes). Or it may be used in a more technical sense to describe the mixture as one of the components of a French **Vermouth**.

MONTILLA (g) 16%

Delicate wine of great distinction which is a first cousin of **Sherry**, though it is not fortified. Made in Andalusia, but inland, near Córdoba, where the hot climate provides grapes with a high sugar content for rapid fermentation. This is carried out in clay jars of an Eastern appearance, a reminder that Córdoba was the capital of Moorish Spain. Montilla is a delightfully Spanish aperitif. In *The World Atlas of Wine*, Hugh Johnson says of these wines: "People claim to find in them the scent of black olives (which are, of course, their perfect partners)."

MOSCATEL (g)

Sweet wine made from the Muscat or Moscato grape, different varieties of which grow throughout southern Europe and the Mediterranean. A particularly fine, scenty moscatel is made in Setúbal, Portugal. The same grape family is used to produce sparkling wines in Italy and California. The fruity wine called Muscadet is made from a quite different grape.

MOW TOY (g) 45%

Malodorous grain spirit made in Hong Kong.

MÜNCHENER (g) 4%+

Term used in many countries for a malty, dark **Lager** beer of the type made famous by Munich brewers in the 1800s. In Germany today, these brews are identified as being *dunkel* (dark) to distinguish them from the *hell* (light) style of malty beer subsequently popularized by the Münchener brewers.

MUSCATELLE, MUSCADELLE

Two common variations on the spelling of **Moscatel**.

"NAPOLÉON" BRANDY

Boney is often invoked to describe a **Cognac** which is at least five years old. Oddly, the Napoléon brandy of a particular house is apt to be its second best rather than its very best. Courvoisier claims that its brandy was laid aside for Napoléon when, after his abdication, he planned to leave secretly for the United States. The house uses "the brandy of Napoléon" as its slogan. Occasionally, auction rooms have sold for substantial sums brandies alleged to date back to the time of Napoléon. No one has ever been able to authenticate the age of these brandies, and there is scant likelihood of their having been around in Napoléon's day. While a brandy of such age would no doubt be of great historical interest, it would be no more mature today than when it was bottled. In glass, brandy does not improve, and in the cask it deteriorates after about 70 years. See also **Mandarine Napoléon**.

NEW ENGLAND RUM (g)

No longer a recognized category. **Rum** was the first spirit distilled in North America, and the industry in New England was the banker of the triangular trade. Some of the rum was taken to Africa and exchanged for slaves, who were then taken to the Caribbean and traded for molasses, which was brought back to New England as a raw material.

NOCINO (g) approx. 30%

A delicious, bitter, Italian digestif made from nuts, with a forgiving hint of sweetness in the aftertaste.

NOILLY PRAT (p) 17%

The best-known French dry vermouth, made in Marseilles. Very dry. Excellent in a Dry Martini cocktail, or as an aperitif with lots of ice and just a little soda. Made with two white wines and 40 herbs, steeped for a year and a half. In Britain, where "French" was once a familiar term for dry vermouth, a famous slogan punningly proposed, "Say Noilly Prat and your French is perfect."

NOYAU, CRÈME DE, sometimes NOYAUX (g) 25–30% ●

Almond-flavored liqueur made from the kernels of peaches, apricots, or other pitted fruits. A rather sweet digestif, also useful in cocktails. Colorless and pink versions, of which the finest is made by the French firm of Veuve Champion.

OKOLEHAO, OKE (g)

A Hawaiian spirit produced from sugar and rice, and flavored with a local root.

OLD TOM GIN (p)

A very old brand of sweetened London gin.

OLOROSO (g) •

The third principal class of **Sherry**, dark and sweet. A dessert wine, or the basis of a good quality sweet sherry. See also **Amoroso**.

ORANGE BITTERS (g) 15%+ •

A very dry essence that is a traditional and valued ingredient in cocktails. Not always easy to find in retail liquor stores, but worth seeking out. Major liqueur houses and gin distillers still make orange bitters.

ORANGE-FLOWER WATER (g) •

Light, non-alcoholic essence originating from France which is used to great effect in some cocktails, notably the Ramos Fizz of New Orleans.

ORANGE LIQUEURS

The most famous are the **Curaçao** family, made from the peel of small green oranges native to the island of that name in the former Dutch West Indies (Netherlands Antilles). Among the different degrees of dryness in curaçao, *triple sec* has become almost a liqueur in its own right, as has its original and most famous producer, the firm **Cointreau**. Dutch and German distillers make Half and Half (g) liqueurs which are a mix of curaçao and various spices and there are many other variations. Another Dutch creation is a citrus and herb liqueur, Pimpeltjens (p), made by De Kuyper. South Africa has a liqueur called **Van der Hum** (g) based on a local variety of tangerine, Italy the excellent brandy-based herbal orange **Aurum**, Belgium its elegant **Mandarine Napoléon**, and there are many more proprietary brands elsewhere in the world.

ORGEAT (g)

A non-alcoholic almond-flavored syrup used in cocktails.

OUZO, sometimes DOUZICO (g) 40%

Well-known popular **Absinthe** substitute from Greece. When diluted with ice and water as is customary with such drinks, ouzo turns white rather than the greeny-yellow of its French cousins. It is also drier.

PARFAIT AMOUR (g) 30%

Perfect love is, it seems, a sweet and sickly experience which is not particularly constant. Though most major liqueur producers, in Europe at least, make perfect love, there seems little agreement about the way in which this is done. Liqueurist Peter Hallgarten reckons it is something like crème de **Violette**, with additional flavor from flower petals, and a sweet citrus base. Perfect love is, he says, scented and slightly spicy. There are those who would argue specifically for orange, flower of cinnamon, and peach pits.

PASHA (p) 25%+

A coffee liqueur which originates from Turkey.

PASTIS (g) 45%

From the French word for mixture, a pastiche of ingredients that provides a more licorice-tasting alternative to **Pernod**. Pastis has a brownish tinge when neat and is paler than Pernod when diluted. There are a number of brands, among which Ricard is the best known. Pastis are especially popular in Provence. Ready-mixed and flavored variations are also marketed. See also **Absinthe**.

PEACH

A reticent but versatile performer at the cocktail bar. Peach bitters are as hard to find as their orangey cousins, and every bit as worthwhile. Persico and variations are distilled from peach leaves and are still to be found in liqueur capitals like Amsterdam and Paris. The French call peach liqueurs Pêche, and other countries have their own versions. Delicious peach is the most pronounced flavor in **Southern Comfort**.

PEPPERMINT SCHNAPPS 20–30%

Increasingly popular in the United States as a much less sweet and lighter-bodied substitute for crème de **Menthe**. "Schnapps" not for its potency but for its base, which is a **Pot still** spirit in the German style.

PEPPERS

In some countries, hot and spicy liqueurs are made from peppers. The best-known example is a traditional spicy vodka from Russia called Okhotnichya (g), 38.5%, in which peppers are a dominant flavoring along with several other spices, herbs, and berries. A homemade version can be created if hot peppers are steeped for several weeks in plain vodka.

PERCOLATION

Process used in the manufacture of liqueurs, in which the spirit base, cold, hot, or in vapor form, is passed through a container filled with the natural flavoring agents, which in this case may be herbs. This process may have to be repeated for weeks or months to achieve the desired level of extraction.

PERNOD (P) 45% ●

The original **Absinthe** substitute, and by far the most famous, though its makers are at persistent pains to proclaim the innocence and individuality of their product. Their elixir is surely safe, and over the years its popularity has remained undented by its local rivals, or such Franco-Americana as Oxygenee and Herbsaint, the latter cleverly pronouncing its antecedence. Drinks of this type are commonly diluted with four to five parts of water, over ice. In the south of France and north of Spain, more especially Provence and Catalonia, they are drunk both as aperitifs and liqueurs with great style. A bar-fitting specially for the Pernod drinker is the water cooler with tiny taps for

---

AMERICAN BEAUTY *RICH-TASTING AND HEADY: BRANDY, DRY VERMOUTH, ORANGE JUICE, PEPPERMINT SCHNAPPS, WITH PORT FLOATING ON TOP.* *SEE PAGE 138.*

the customer, such as is found not only in southern Europe but also in certain Francophile haunts in London and New Orleans. Another refinement is a funnel that rests atop a glass of neat Pernod or pastis. A cube of sugar is placed over the hole in the funnel, and ice is packed on top. Water is then poured into the funnel and allowed to drip slowly through ice and sugar into the drink.

PERRIER (P) ●

Hannibal is believed to have refreshed himself with Perrier; the Romans built baths at the spring, which is near Nîmes, in the south of France; and it was Napoléon III who decreed that the waters should be bottled and made available "for the good of France." The spring was first commercially exploited by A. W. St.-John Harmsworth, of the London newspaper dynasty, who bought the source as a gift to his tutor, a Dr. Perrier, who was a collector of such things. Harmsworth, an enthusiast for sport and gymnastics who was later crippled in a road accident in France, suggested that the Perrier bottle be shaped like an Indian club. All of this happened long before Perrier was given the stamp of approval by New Yorkers as "the power drink," and that with the addition of lime juice. Though there are those who would argue against the use of mineral-tasting waters in mixed drinks, the edge of Perrier offsets the stickiness of fruit juices, and it also does interesting things to the taste of gin. Such playful behavior aside, Perrier more than any other mineral water can stand alone as a drink of considerable character. It has the useful attribute through its alkaline composition of being both a digestif and a speedy soother of hangovers, yet its seeming saltiness is so slight as not to impair its quenching qualities whatever.

PERSICO (G) see Peach

PETRUS BOONEKAMP (P) see Boonekamp

PÉYCHAUD (P) see Bitters

PILSENER (g) 4.25–5.25%

The world's best-known beer style. The original was first brewed in 1842 at Pilsen, in Bohemia, now a part of the Czech Republic. With its flowery aroma, its (then novel) golden color, its soft maltiness, hoppy dryness, and digestif qualities, it became the most popular of the new bottom-fermented beers, which were the toast of German-speaking Europe. Like its counterpart in Budweis, and its contemporaries in Vienna and Munich, it was widely imitated, and its celebrity was taken to the New World in the Hungry Forties by German émigrés, later to be the founders of the modern American brewing industry. Only the original brewery is legally entitled to call its product Pilsner Urquell (p). The prefix means "the original source of." Most imitators use the spelling Pilsener. See **Lager**.

PIMENTO

The dried aromatic berries of the Jamaica pepper tree are used to make a liqueur in the Caribbean and elsewhere in the Americas.

PIMM'S (P) 31.5%

Unique form of English gin. A flavored gin or a sling? See page 200.

PINEAU DE CHARENTES (g) 17%

Sweetish, bland but agreeable and substantial aperitif made in its own appellation contrôlée region of the Cognac country by the blending of surplus brandy with fresh grape juice in a ratio of two to one. The best Pineau is aged in wood. It is served very cold, and can be reinforced with vodka or a drying calvados. Pineau is the Charentais form of **Ratafia**. See also **Mistelle**.

PISCO (g) 45% •

Perhaps the next hot spirit, inexorable as the fashions of drinking now are. Pisco is a brandy made from Muscat wine and matured for a short time in clay jars. Traditionally, it has a taste and aroma of beeswax, and is made in **Pot stills**. Pisco is the Quechua word for bird, the name of the tribe which once made beeswax-coated amphorae in which to transport the brandy, and of the port in Peru from which it is shipped. Chile also claims to have a tradition of this type of brandy, though it uses an Italian grape. The drink is also common in Bolivia. Pisco began to gain popularity in some parts of the United States in the late 1960s and early 1970s, and a popular brand is Inca (p), with its Indian-head bottle. The Pisco Punch, which is really a sour, has contributed greatly to the popularity of this once-primitive spirit.

PLYMOUTH GIN (g) 40%

Gin came from Leiden to Plymouth, and so did the Pilgrim fathers, on their way to the New World. Sadly for mythology, no connection has ever been made. What is established is that gin crossed the sea with fighting men, and Plymouth is historically the home of the Royal Navy. Legend decrees that it was the Navy who first mixed gin with Angostura bitters, an elixir invented by a military doctor in the Caribbean as a cure for tropical ills. Today Pink Gin (see page 201) is still properly made with Plymouth gin. Plymouth traditionally emphasized orris, which gave it a more aromatic and oily character than **London Dry gin**. Over the years, the distillers have gradually ditched distinctiveness in favor of world-wide acceptability, and made their gin more like the internationally famous London version. Despite this foolish faintheartedness, they still make a gin which is distinctively smooth, perhaps because they use natural water from Dartmoor.

POIRE WILLIAMS, WILLIAMINE (g) 45%

The bottle growing on the tree is the astonishing novelty that helps this excellent **Eau-de-vie** capture the attention of even the most unimaginative drinker. The bottle is attached to the tree so that a pear will grow inside. When both are picked, the remaining space inside the bottle is filled with a brandy made from the same fruit, the Williams pear, otherwise known as the Bartlett. Such an elaborate

EMERALD *ONE FOR ENVIRONMENTALISTS? ENTIRELY GREEN, EVEN DOWN TO THE CHERRY, BASED ON GIN AND CRÈME DE MENTHE. SEE PAGE 168.*

performance is more than a form of folk advertising; the pear in the bottle beautifully brings out the fine orchard bouquet of this blossoming brandy. The most fragrant bottle plantations are said to be in Switzerland.

POMERANZ (g)

Old northern European liqueur or bitters based on unripe oranges.

PONCHE (g)

A "punch" liqueur from Spain, brandy based, with the flavor of sherry.

PORT (g) 17% •

Vinho do Porto, to give it its full name, which it must be accorded in some countries, including the United States, as a precaution against imitation. Port is the wine of Oporto, and the fortified wine of Portugal. Oporto is a port city in both senses of the word. It stands at the mouth of the River Douro; upstream, in rough hill country, lie the vineyards. Port wine dates from the time when the Portuguese were given trade preference by the English. The Portuguese are still described by the English as "our oldest allies," and the friendship dates back to that time. In 1703 the English were at war with France, so they took their thirst and their trade to Portugal, which agreed in return to buy British wool. The agreement, known as the Methuen Treaty after the English ambassador, overlooked the fact that Portuguese wine was hardly to the taste of people accustomed to French wines. Thus the English invented port, just as they popularized almost every other fortified wine.

The wines of the Douro are fortified by the addition of local brandy, which arrests fermentation prematurely, leaving a sweetening of grape sugar in the wine. The least sweet of ports is the kind made from various white grapes. The French, who are today's biggest consumers of port, use the white version as an aperitif. They accord the same treatment to a run-of-the-mill red port, which is occasionally still found in an English pub as a winter drink, sometimes served in a mix with brandy or, in summer, long – with ice and lemonade. Pub port is often the kind called Ruby, as if it were a barmaid, dark, rather rough, matured in wood but not for very long. A Tawny port, which should look as it sounds and be comparatively dry, has been matured in wood for a very respectable period. It goes well with nuts at Christmas, or stilton cheese at any available opportunity. All of these ports are blended, and aged in wood, in which habitat they mature more quickly than in the bottle. A "late-bottled vintage" or "porto of the vintage" is an unblended wine that has been aged in wood. A "vintage-character" port is intended to be laid down to mature in the bottle. As it does so, sediment will throw a "crust" on the side of the bottle. In order that the crust will not break and mix with the wine, the bottle has to be handled with great care, and decanted before the port can be served. A vintage port is an unblended wine from an exceptional year. It is not for drinking, rather for keeping and bequeathing. "Eventually," promises Hugh Johnson, "perhaps after 20 years, it will have a fatness and fragrance, richness and delicacy which is incomparable."

The many uses to which port is put testify to the political need of the English all those years ago to buy as much of the stuff as possible. It remains, above all, the after-dinner drink of the academic, the silk, and the gentleman. Here it has yet another use to the Englishman, for it provides the litmus test of breeding. If he is a true gentleman, he will, at the dinner table, always pass the decanter clockwise.

POT STILL

An important distinction in the production of any spirit is the type of still used: pot or continuous? Only the pot still is used in the production of **Malt Scotch whisky** (in which beverage it is desirous to retain the flavor and bouquet of both the barley and the peat) and **Cognac** (where the character of the grape and its soil survive). The pot still is used in the production of fruit **Eaux-de-vie** and dark **Jamaica rums** and any other spirit which is intended to retain the pungency and personality of its source. This lofty aim is achieved through the stumbling, inefficient, and un-thorough way in which the pot still distils. A pot still is characterful and individualistic, and so are its products. It is an old-fashioned still, with a familiar appearance, a pear-shaped "pot" (usually copper), in which the materials to be distilled are heated, and a "swan's neck" carrying their vapor to the condenser. It is a fat raconteur, which tells the stories of the materials it distils. Each distillation is a separate operation, after which it has to stop and be recharged. If it got on with its work, if it were more efficient, it would produce a much purer distillate, which would have less flavor. That sort of work is carried out by the cost-effective, businesslike, upright Patent Continuous Column still (it is described by any of those self-explanatory adjectives, or by the name of Coffey, one of its several inventors, along with Stein and various Frenchmen). The **Continuous still** is efficient, thorough, controllable, versatile, but lacking in idiosyncrasy. It makes grain whiskeys, light rums, and neutral spirit for vodkas and some liqueurs. In the case of **London Dry gin**, the neutral spirit base is made in a continuous still but the botanicals are distilled in a pot still.

POTEEN various spellings (g)

The word is a diminutive for pot, and has nothing to do with potatoes. They may have been used from time to time; in Ireland it would be surprising if they weren't, but accounts of illicit distillation usually refer to the use of malted barley and perhaps oats. Though every spirit-drinking nation has a tradition of illicit distillation and battles with the authorities, the Irish are better story-tellers than most. There have even been a number of legitimate poteens, if that is not a contradiction in terms, but didn't the Scots produce canned Scotch mist for sale to English and American tourists? Anything goes, as the song says. See **Irish whiskey**.

PRUNELLE

French name for the sloe berry, which is made into an eau-de-vie and a liqueur in Alsace and the Loire. See **Eau-de-vie**.

PUERTO RICAN RUM (g) 40%+

Light-bodied, like the rum of most Spanish-speaking islands, and produced in a **Continuous still**. The best known label is **Bacardi**, formerly of Cuba.

PULQUE (g)

The drink of the Aztecs, and still popular in Mexico. Pulque is the fermented juice or sap of the mezcal plant. When invading Spaniards brought with them the art of distillation (newly learned from the Moors?), it became possible to convert the ferocious fermentation into a spirit, today known as mezcal unless it happens to be produced in or around the town of Tequila. See **Mezcal** and **Tequila**.

PUNCH

Not only a spiced alcoholic, mixed drink served to a group of people from a bowl, and often containing rum, but also a bottled version of the same thing which has become a national drink in Sweden. See **Swedish punsch**.

PUNT E MES (p) 17%

Delicious and distinctive Milanese aperitif in the **Vermouth** style. Very full flavor with an orangey sweetness playing against a quinine bitterness. Its rich color merges the reddish hue of other aperitifs with more of a brown tinge, and it has a slightly syrupy consistency that is delightfully offset by a small swoosh of soda, three or four big ice cubes and a slice of lemon. In Italy it is often mixed with orange juice. A particular mix gave rise to the name, a Milanese stockbroker's way of saying "a point and a half."

QUETSCH (g) 45%

One of the great **Eaux-de-vie**, distilled from the small, sour, bluish-purple quetsch or Switzen plum.

RAKI (g) 40–45%

Most commonly used in Turkey, where it usually means the local **Absinthe** substitute, which is of the very dry, white type. Also used to describe any hard liquor in the Levant and points east, since it is a variation on **Arak**.

RATAFIA (g)

A word that has meant a variety of different drinks at different times and places, though always a mélange of sorts. It seems to have derived from the Creole word for rum, and perhaps it thus fell into currency during the time of French sea power. It is also said to have been used to describe a liqueur drunk at the ratification of treaties, and perhaps was flavored with nuts and fruits. A ratafia has been a flavored version of a North African, notably Algerian, wine, and it has been also a punch-type product of the town of Grenoble. Given the geographical location of Grenoble, the latter is likely originally to have been a fruit-and-herb vermouth, which might explain today's meaning. One ingredient of a vermouth is a **Mistelle** which is a blending of fresh grape juice with brandy. The word mistelle is also used colloquially to describe the same sort of mixture served as a drink in its own right, and that potion is known generically as ratafia, especially in the Champagne area, where it is sometimes flavored with different fruits. The same drink is made in the Charentes region but there it is called **Pineau**.

RECTIFICATION

The purification of spirit by redistillation. Potash salts are also added for this purpose.

RETSINA

The unmistakable wine of Greece, with a powerfully resinous palate from which many a drinker shrinks at first taste but grows to love. About half the wine produced in Greece is resinated, notably that from Attica, the region of Athens, and it is available in both white and rosé versions. It is not a Balkan drink but a Greek one, and apparently has been since ancient times. Hugh Johnson says: "Traces of pine resin have been found in amphorae from earliest times.... It is usually assumed that it was used to preserve the wine, but resinated wine does not age well. There is reason enough in the fresh, sappy, turpentine-like flavor which resin gives if added during fermentation. The result is one of the most individual and appetizing of all drinks."

RHUM

French word for **Rum** – usually indicating a medium-bodied version.

RIESLING

The best German grape, "fine, fragrant, fruity," in the words of Hugh Johnson. Very extensively used in Germany, and the grape of the great and often expensive hocks.

RIOJA (g)

The wine-producing region which in Spain has the position of honor elsewhere conferred on Bordeaux and Burgundy. Rioja's best wines are its reds, a very pale version called *clarete* (like the French *clairet*), a dry version in a shouldered Bordeaux-style bottle, and a fuller version in a sloping-shouldered Burgundy-style bottle. Growers from Bordeaux came to Rioja in the 1870s, refugees from phylloxera until it caught up with them, but they implanted their techniques in Spain. Rioja wines are aged for a long time in wood, which lightens and smoothens the reds but can flatten the palate of the whites.

ROCK AND RYE (g) 30–35%

Originally rock candy crystallized in rye whiskey. Today rock candy syrup is used, with rye, grain, neutral spirits, and sometimes various fruits.

RON

The Spanish word for **Rum**. Spanish rums are usually light.

ROSÉ

Pink, as always in wines and recently in a medium vermouth.

ROSE, CRÈME DE (g) 30%

Delicate rose-petal liqueur made with vanilla and sometimes citrus oils.

ROSSI

An Italian family which went into business with the **Martinis** to produce a famous **Vermouth**. Bitter Rossi (p) 25% is a delightful pink, vermouth-style patent aperitif from the same house.

ROSSO

Italian word for red, as applied to the Rosso (g) style of **Vermouth**. This is sweet, but less so than the **Bianco**. Rosso is the original Italian style of vermouth and remains the most popular in Italy.

RUM (g) 40–75.5% •

All spirits put notions into men's minds, and inspire mythology, but none more than rum, the very origins of which are lost in the smoke of cannon, the clatter of swords, and the clamor of mainbraces being spliced. It was the first national drink of the New World, the United States included, and the mythology says that the maritime frontiersmen sailed there on a sea of rum. No one is sure, amid the excitement, where the first rum was produced, or how it got its name. There is evidence to suggest that the name derives from a word in the dialect of maritime Devon, but it may just as well come from French, Spanish, or even the Latin *saccharum*, meaning sugar. It was an Italian, none other than Christopher Columbus, who introduced sugar cane to the Caribbean, and almost every European nation involved itself in the West Indies. The Dutch even took rum to the East Indies (it became the first national spirit of Australia, too), and a Javanese version returned as a popular import to Sweden. The Scandinavians were also involved in the Caribbean, and a formerly Danish town now plays an important part in the German rum trade, where drinkers have a choice of the real thing or a rum-flavored *Verschnitt*. Each colonizing nation had its own different procedures for the production of rum, in addition to which each territory's soil and climate has its own influence. Until the 1920s, the French regarded the three principal procedures as

---

BETWEEN THE SHEETS *AN OLD CLASSIC. COINTREAU, BRANDY, AND WHITE RUM, WITH LIME JUICE OPTIONAL.* *SEE PAGE 143.*

producing quite different drinks, and gave each a separate name. Today, it is all rum (or *ron*, or *rhum*, according to ethnicity). Nor can the name of an island or Latin American country be used to indicate a style of rum unless the product was actually made there. Although each rum country has its own traditional type, many today also mimic the styles of their competitors.

Rum can be produced from two different raw materials: it can be distilled directly from the fermented juice of crushed sugar cane; or the sugar itself can first be extracted, and the rum made from the molasses which remain. A further variation entails the addition of dunder (residue from a previous distillation) to make a more pungent rum. Whichever raw materials are used, the duration of fermentation will also influence the final taste of the product. Then there is the means of distillation, since both pot and continuous stills are used. Traditionally, the French-speaking countries use the **Pot still** to distil cane juice, on some occasions with dunder, into a high-quality rum of medium body. Among the English-speaking countries, Jamaica traditionally produces full-bodied rums from molasses and dunder in pot stills; Guyana produces its own distinctive style known as Demerara, which is dark but medium-bodied, thanks to rapid fermentation using molasses in **Continuous stills**; Barbados uses both types of still to make its distinctively soft and smoky rum; and Trinidad produces medium-light rums in continuous stills. The Spanish-speaking countries produce light-bodied rums from molasses in continuous stills. Light-bodied rums do not require extensive aging, those with a medium or full body may be matured in charred oak casks for anything from two to 15 years.

RYE (g) 40–50% •

The first whiskey of the United States, probably dating back to the 1600s, though no one can be sure. Settlers from Scotland and Ireland had difficulty in growing good malting barley in their new homeland, but they had less trouble with rye. The Irish, at least, were already accustomed to using that in the production of whiskey. Those first distillers produced for themselves and their friends, and not on a commercial scale, and whiskey was not the significant spirit in the United States at that time; rum was. Rye was the tipple of the

Pennsylvania and Maryland settlers, and it is still associated with those states. Sometimes, though, it seems that rye has never quite recovered from being upstaged by Kentucky **Bourbon**, which came later. That the first whiskey in the history of the United States should be relegated to being very much the second in public taste is a shame. Perhaps because it was the whiskey of the first settlers, rye has always lacked the glamour of bourbon. Perhaps because it has such character, with the spicy, almost minty, flavors conferred by the rye grain, it has been mistakenly thought to be unsophisticated. Nor have American distillers and their marketing men helped by using such a confusion of semi-technical terms with which to describe the styles of their whiskeys. It is easy for drinkers to forget what is really what, and to neglect the fact that the United States offers them the choice of two distinct and distinctive indigenous whiskeys. Rye whiskey must be made with at least 51% of the grain from which it takes its name, the rest being corn and barley, and is distilled in a continuous still. Like bourbon, it must be aged in new charred oak barrels for not less than a year, though in practice it is likely to be matured for much longer.

ST.-RAPHAËL (P) 17%

The sweetest of the major French patent aperitifs, in which some drinkers claim to detect a delectable hint of peaches.

SAKE, SAKI (g) 14–18%

Not a spirit, though it is drunk short and tastes quite strong; not really a wine, though it is commonly described as rice wine; technically a beer, though that is what it least resembles. This ancient drink from Japan is not distilled; nor is it made from grapes; it is fermented, from rice. Sake is normally served quite warm, because heat releases its considerable bouquet. *Grossman's Guide* recommends the following procedure: "Place the opened bottle in a pot of boiling water. Remove it when the sake is about 100 to 105 degrees Fahrenheit. Decant the warm sake into small ceramic bottles called tokkuri. Pour into tiny porcelain bowls called sakazuki. The sake should be sipped. Often these sakazuki have a little tube on the outside, so that as you sip you draw in air and produce a whistling sound."

SAMBUCA (g) approx. 40% •

The flambé is the fun of sambuca. First float three or four coffee beans on top of a glass full of sambuca, then apply a flame to the liqueur. Let the flame dance for a few minutes until the coffee beans have sizzled and roasted, releasing an extra aroma into the sambuca, then blow it out as if it were candles on a cake. If you want to be really showy, lower the lights in the room before your performance, and explain to your guest(s) that the Italians say sambuca with coffee beans is *"con mosche"* – "with flies."

For the lazy or modest, there is a variation of sambuca that comes already infused with coffee. Instead of being colorless, it is a dark brown, and labelled *negra*. Since the sharpness of the coffee offsets the stickiness of the sambuca, it is, as usual, deliciously indulgent to be lazy. There are many coffee liqueurs prepared to do double duty after dinner, but none quite as interesting as sambuca negra. Although it is a cousin of the French and Spanish sweet anis liqueurs, sambuca is made by an extraction method that provides a notably drier palate, and its distinctive ingredient is that of the elderbush. In its own country, sambuca is currently rather out of style. It is to be hoped that this foolish neglect stems merely from a temporary case of a prophet being without honor.

SAUTERNES (g)

Just as Le Montrachet is the most famous white wine of Burgundy, so is Sauternes of Bordeaux, but there is a catch. Ordinary Sauternes is just another white wine, a pleasant drink for either before or after a meal, so long as it is served very cold. Only the famous châteaux, among which the most glittering, of course, is Château d'Yquem, can afford to make true Sauternes, that fabulously rich – and fabulously priced – sweet white wine, in the traditional way. To do this, it is necessary to pick over the vineyard as often as eight or nine times, to seek out those individual grapes blessed at various times through the months of September to December with the so-called Noble Rot. Only these wizened grapes have the unctuous, sweet, scenty intensity which makes a true Sauternes. Even then, it is only in the best of years that this will be possible.

SCHNAPPS (g)

To the rest of the world, schnapps vaguely means a "white" hard liquor drunk in northern Europe, perhaps a grainy-tasting shot which is taken very cold in a short glass. The Dutch firm of **Bols** even makes such a drink under the name of Aromatic Schnapps (p) in some markets, though the term is more commonly associated with Germany. There, usually spelled with only one p, schnaps is an omnibus term for any hard liquor. If asked for a schnaps, a German bartender would either reel off a list of choices, or serve what he calls a **Korn** (g). This too, is a vague term, but it usually refers to a clear grain spirit of excellent quality that has been distilled in a **Pot still** in a manner intended to retain some of the flavor of the raw material and that may have been matured by aging. If the bartender offers a **Steinhäger** or wacholder (g), he is referring to a spirit of this type that has been redistilled with crushed juniper berries, a splendid German version of gin. The korn spirit and its juniper brother, both being clear, are jointly bracketed as "klarer," and this is another term used by bartenders in Germany, and by drinkers when ordering. While **Klarer** are most often the products of northern Germany, the original wacholder gin coming from the town of Steinhägen in the province of Westphalia, a request for schnapps elsewhere in the country might even elicit offers of a brandy from the Rhine or **Kirschwasser** from the Black Forest.

SCOTCH (g) ●

A whisky made only in Scotland – never in England. Inside each bottle are the flavors of Scotland: the snow-melt from the Grampians; the clean granite, sandstone, or ironstone through which the water seeped and rose; the peaty moorlands, heather, clover, or ferns through which it passed; the salty sea-breezes; and seaweedy coasts where it matured. A **Single malt** will have the character of one specific location. A **Vatted malt** will combine perhaps half a dozen, but uses no grain whisky.

A **Blended** Scotch contains anything from a dozen to 40 malts, and two or three grain whiskies. The aim of vatting and blending is to achieve consistency and to balance sweetness with dryness, floweriness with smokiness, saltiness with spiciness. Even deluxe blends may contain as much as 60% of the less expensive grain whisky. Scotch whisky is distilled at around 70% alcohol, reduced with local water to around 60 for maturation, then again to 43 or 40 for packaging, often at a central bottling hall in the Lowlands of Scotland. Whisky exported in bulk will be reduced in the importing country, with denatured local water.

SEAGRAM (p)

The name of a whisky firm in Ontario, Canada, bought by the late Samuel Bronfman in 1926. By the early 1950s, Bronfman had made Seagram's into the world's biggest distilling group, and moved into a much-acclaimed new headquarters building, designed by Mies van der Rohe, in New York. Seagram's brands include Chivas Regal and, since 1977, The **Glenlivet**.

SEC, SECO, SECCO (g)

The words meaning dry in French, Spanish, and Italian respectively.

SEKT (g)

Nothing to do with dryness. Sekt is a generic term for German sparkling wines, many of which are fruitily sweet. Dry Sekt is labelled Trocken.

SHERRY (g) 15–18% •

One of the world's fine wines and great aperitifs in its inimitable **Fino** form, and a richly versatile drink as an **Amontillado** or **Oloroso**. It is only a true sherry if it is made in the Jerez region, though other countries hyphenate the style. Jerez de la Frontera is in the province of Cadiz, in Andalusia, southern Spain. In the course of its history, it has variously been known as Jerez, Xeres, Saris, Sherisch, Sherris, and, especially by the English, Sherry. The wine that bears its name is fortified with brandy and is distinguished by two unusual processes in its production. One is a fermentation brought about by the action of an unusual yeast, *flor*, which forms a film on the surface of the wine. *Flor* can live in higher amounts of alcohol than other yeasts, and it imparts a special flavor to the wine. The other distinctive aspect of sherry production is the system of aging and blending. In the bodega, the wine is kept in ranks of wooden butts, anything from 20 to 100 in number, and is transferred from one to another by jug until it has passed through the whole system, which is known as a solera. At one end of the system, young wine is added; at the other end, mature wine is drawn. Since all the wine in the system is of the same category, it is further blended during the ensuing processes which take place before shipping. The production of sherry is complex, painstaking, and infinitely subtle; when the Moors nurtured viniculture in southern Spain a thousand years ago, they did a service to the world.

SHRUB (g)

A homemade drink produced by the maceration of fruits in alcohol (see page 208), and a patent cordial of low alcoholic content from the west of England.

SINGLE MALT (g)

A **Malt whisky** that is the product of just one distillery, though the bottling may comprise more than one production run.

SLIVOVITZ

various spellings (g) 40–50%

Distinctive style of good-quality plum brandy made in various countries of central Europe and the Balkans, and was regarded as the national spirit of the former Yugoslavia. Sadly it was not strong enough to hold the country together. Slivovitz is made from the large sweet Pozega plum of Bosnia, and the trees are not cropped for this purpose until they are a mature 20 years old. Part of the kernel is used, producing a characteristically dry almond bitterness and oiliness which some drinkers find unpleasant, but which on the tongues of central European connoisseurs is likely to prompt cries of *Na Zdorov'e* or *Mazeltov!* A further characteristic of Slivovitz, which distinguishes it from the equally admirable plum brandies of the **Eau-de-vie** country, is the method of aging. Slivovitz is aged in wood, hence its yellowish color with a tinge of brown.

SLOE GIN (g) 25%+

A very English and rather rural drink for the flasks of fox-hunting folk. A **Gin** because that is what the sloe berries, and sometimes other fruit flavorings, are macerated in. Sloe gin is matured in wood.

SOUR MASH (g)

Although this process is proclaimed strongly on the label of **Jack Daniel's** excellent product, a sour mash is used by many American distillers in the production of **Bourbon**. The residue from a previous fermentation is added to the new mash to assist continuity of character and reinforce the flavor and bouquet.

SOUTHERN COMFORT (P) 50% ●

One of the few indigenous American liqueurs, and surely the oldest. Said to have been derived from a cocktail of peaches and **Bourbon**, which was in turn invented either in New Orleans or in St.-Louis, Missouri, where Southern Comfort is made. It took Southern Comfort a while to cross the Mason-Dixon line, but it is now a hot drink all over the world. In addition to the peaches, it has a hint of oranges and herbs, and it is relatively dry and strong for a liqueur. More of a flavored whiskey, suitable for sunny afternoons in mixed drinks and early evenings on the rocks, though some drinkers like it after dinner.

SPANISH BRANDIES (g) 40%

In Europe, the consensus would probably say that Spanish brandy, in its own rather ebullient way, is second only to French, though it lacks the pedigree of **Armagnac** or the finesse of **Cognac**. It is sweeter than either, deceptively and dangerously heavy, but at its best very smooth. Though they are in most cases distilled from the wines of La Mancha, around Valdepeñas, south of Madrid, Spanish brandies are often matured and marketed by the sherry shippers of Jerez.

SANGRIA *THE HOLIDAY AND BARBEQUE FAVORITE: SPANISH RED WINE AND BRANDY DRESSED UP WITH CURAÇAO, ORANGE, AND LEMON JUICE.* *SEE PAGE 205.*

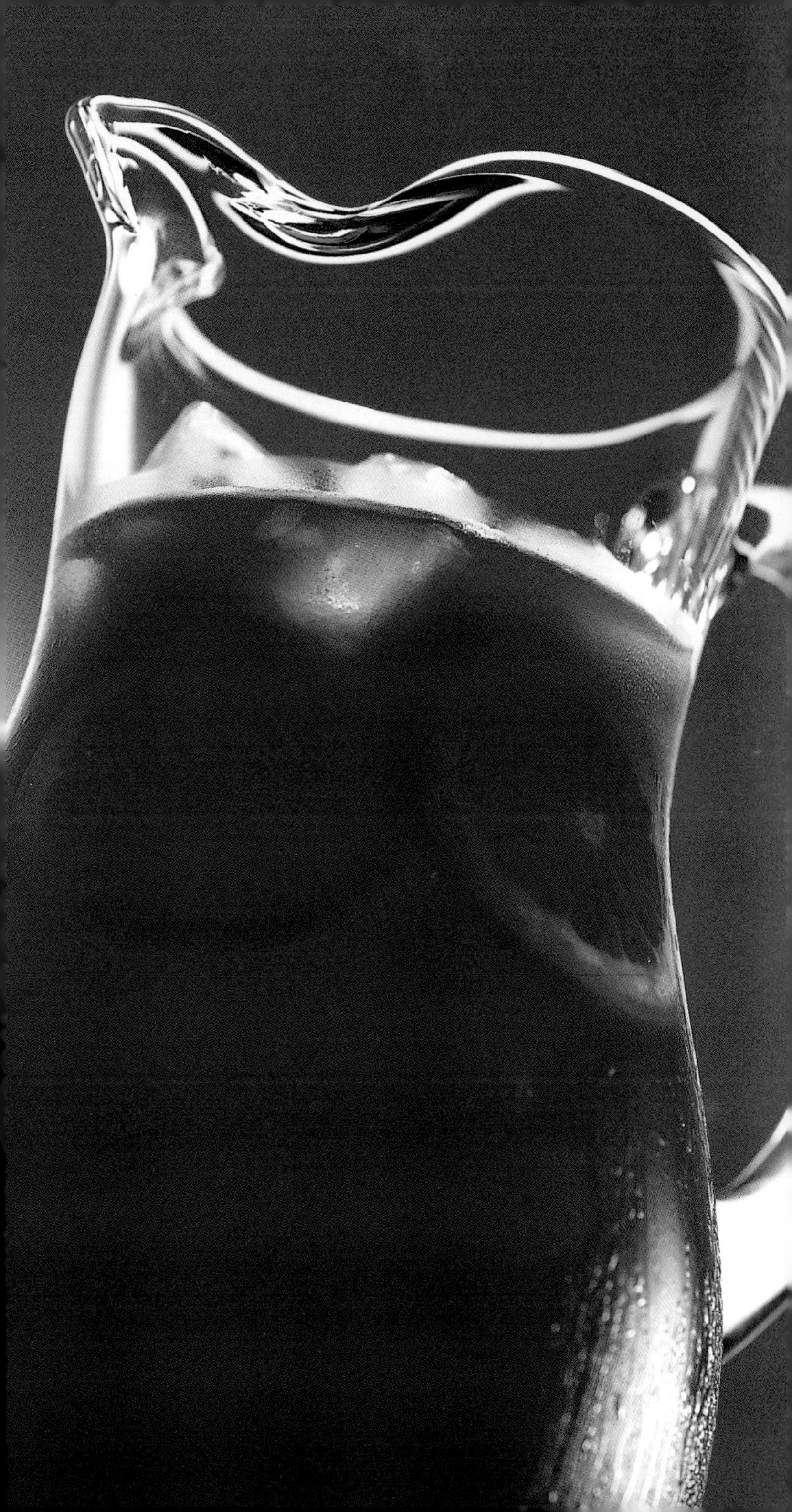

SPUMANTE (g)

Italian term for sparkling wine. See **Asti**.

STEAM BEER (g) approx. 5%

The term "Steam Brewery" found its way onto labels when this source of power was first used. "Steam Beer" is a more specific reference to a style made by an improvised method during the California gold rush. This used lager yeast but at ale temperatures, due to the lack of ice. It was a lively beer, and the hiss of pressure when the casks were tapped was said to resemble steam. The style is continued by the justifiably famous Anchor Steam Beer (p).

STEINHÄGER (g) 30–35%

Excellent German **Gin** made by a most unusual method. Crushed juniper berries are made into a mash and fermented, then distilled. The resultant spirit is then redistilled with neutral alcohol in a **Pot still**. No botanical flavorings are used other than a small quantity of dried juniper berries, which is added in a manner rather reminiscent of the dry-hopping of beer. Despite the use of the berries as both a fermentable material and a flavoring, their influence in the palate of the end product is surprisingly subtle. The product is commonly ordered as Steinhäger, after the town in Westphalia where it traditionally is made, though its generic name is wacholder.

STONSDORFER (p) 32%

A good-quality digestif bitters from Germany.

STOUT (g) 3–7.5%

A top-fermented beer made with highly roasted, sometimes unmalted, barley. Stouts are brewed on a small scale elsewhere in the world, most commonly found in the British Isles, where a clear distinction is made between the sweet type of low alcoholic content such as England's Mackeson (p) and the stronger dry type such as Ireland's Guinness (p).

STREGA (p) 40% •

When two people drink strega they are forever united, according to one of those legends that so conveniently cobweb the liqueur houses of Italy. It is a magic drink, from a recipe created by beautiful maidens who, for reasons unexplained, disguised themselves as witches. This typically Italian liqueur, sweet and spicy, made from more than 70 herbs, is none the worse for its mythology. It is a rich after-dinner drink, useful in cocktails, and the flavoring in a famous Italian ice cream.

SUZE (p) 17%+

Extremely idiosyncratic French bitter aperitif, yellow, with a powerful flavor of gentian root. Drunk with lots of ice, soda, and sometimes lemon juice, or straight by the brave.

SWEDISH PUNSCH (g) 30%

One of the odder drinks in the Western world, though its origins are Eastern. In a throwback to the days when the northern Europeans traded extensively with the East Indies, the Swedes still drink as a local speciality a ready-made punch based on the rum-type arak of Java. What the Swedes term simply punsch is a ready-bottled mélange of **Arak**, neutral spirit, and various wines, aged for some months. The Swedes drink this hot with their winter pea soup or as a liqueur.

TARRAGONA

Town and region in Catalonia famous for several types of fortified wine.

TENNESSEE WHISKEY see **Jack Daniel's**

TEQUILA (g) 40%+ •

Determinedly fashionable spirit. Its potential as both a hard liquor of ritualistic machismo and a cocktail base seems far from exhausted. The sun will continue to rise, Margarita will continue to bestow her salty kisses, but there is surely much more to come. Tequila itself took a long time in coming. The first recorded shipment across the border was in 1873. The tax records of the town of Tequila say that three barrels of "mezcal wine" were sent from Mexico to New Mexico. Tequila was also taken home by the American troops who fought in the 1916 clash, though their adversary Pancho Villa was himself a fanatical teetotaller. The spirit certainly crossed the border during the Prohibition period, too, and began to gain a tiny cult following in the United States during the post-war period, especially the 1950s. The Californians might well argue on historical grounds that tequila has always been their national spirit, and it was students in Los Angeles who made the drink fashionable in the late 1960s. Its broader popularity came with a concerted commercial effort, but the brands which paved the way for that success were sadly bland by Mexican standards. This says more about the neutrality of American taste than it does about the lack of sophistication in the Mexican distilling industry, though the urbane cocktail-mixer David Embury argues that the purpose of the salt-and-lime routine is to counteract the ripe odor of basic tequila. Surely the ritual has more to do with the refreshment of body and soul on a hot, dry day, a continuous process which renders meaningless and interminable arguments as to which is the proper order in which to proceed. Suck a lime, knock back a tequila, and lick the pinch of salt which you have placed on the back of your hand. Now try it while chewing tobacco. Some find the taste of tequila reminiscent of tobacco, others of dill, broccoli, or artichokes (perhaps the last because of that vegetable's visual resemblance to the agave bulb, whose fermented sugars are distilled in **Pot still**s to make the spirit).

The best tequilas are made only from agave. By law, 51% is the minimum, with the remainder made up from cane or other sugar. Some tequilas are matured for only a few weeks, and others colored with caramel to suggest age. Some are flavored with almond essence. Those labelled *Reposado* have been matured in oak tanks for up to six months. Those with the appellation **Añejo** have been kept for at least a year, often two or three, and occasionally eight to ten, in oak barrels, usually former bourbon vessels.

TEQUILA SUNRISE *THE MOST IMPRESSIVE-LOOKING COCKTAIL: TEQUILA, ORANGE JUICE WITH DEEP RED GRENADINE CREATING THE SUNRISE EFFECT.* *SEE PAGE 211.*

TIA MARIA (p) 30%+

An old, established coffee liqueur based on rum, and flavored with Jamaican spices. Made in Jamaica with Blue Mountain coffee, and drier than **Kahlúa**.

TOKAY

Various spellings, and various meanings, the original of which is a famous strong, sweet, white wine made in a small area around the village of Tokaj, in Hungary. Tokay is made from Furmint grapes, and the Noble Rot plays a part, as it does in **Sauternes**. The finest Tokay has been known to mature for 250 years. The word Tokay is also the name of an unrelated grape originating from Algeria, and a blended dessert wine made in California with a sherry flavor.

TRIPLE SEC (g) 30–40%

Not as dry as it sounds, but one of the most refined forms of **Curaçao**.

VAN DER HUM (g) 30%

South African liqueur made from local naartje tangerines, with herbs.

VANDERMINT (p) 30%

Mint chocolate liqueur produced in the Netherlands and marketed in Delft-style bottles.

VANILLA

The beans are occasionally used in mixed drinks. **Crème de** vanille is a smooth and rich liqueur.

VATTED MALT WHISKY (g) 40–57%

Scottish term for **Whisky** blended only from **Single malts**, with no grain. Examples include Strathconon and Glenleven.

VERMOUTH (g) 16–18% •

From the German *wermut*, meaning wormwood, though none of the misconceived odium aimed at **Absinthe** has affected this innocent Franco-Italian genre of aperitif. Within a glass of vermouth is the whole history of alcoholic confection. First and foremost, it is the ultimate in treated wine, and that is a product which dates back to the ancients; there still survives equipment used by the Romans to aromatize their wines, both as a means of improving their flavor and for preservation. Then again, vermouth is the ultimate in complicated herbal recipes. The countless herbs used in vermouths include all the great favorites that occur in bitters (often made by the same companies) and in liqueurs: camomile in dry vermouth, gentian in red, vanilla in sweet, along with Chinese rhubarb, iris root, quinine, citrus peels, and at least 150 others. Somehow the craft survived through the Dark Ages and reappeared in the hands of monks, alchemists, and doctors.

Herbal remedies have never ceased to be widely used in France and more especially Italy, and the shop that supplies the roots, bark, seeds, berries, and flowers sells them equally to the home physic and the domestic liqueurist. Though many of the typical ingredients are obtainable only from the Far East and Latin America, many others grow in the Alps. It was there, on both sides of the mountain ranges, and either side of the Franco-Italian frontier, that the production of liqueurs and vermouths, especially the latter, became an industry: in France, at Chambéry, famous for dry, delicate vermouths, at Lyons, whence **Noilly** moved to Marseilles, still not far from the Alps, and at Grenoble; in Italy, at Turin, the biggest vermouth-producing city of all, home of both **Martini** and **Cinzano**, and at Milan, where the term vermouth was invented by Carpano. Each is still made in a slightly different way, though all are macerated, for periods of six months to a year or more. Some are partially the product of distillation, notably the dry type, which is the strongest. All are extensively used in cocktails, and as aperitifs, usually with plenty of ice, and sometimes soda.

VICHY CÉLESTINS (p)

Famous salty mineral water from the French spa town of Vichy, north of Clermont Ferrand. If water can be dry, Vichy is.

VIEILLE CURE (p) 43%

Well known for its "stained glass" packaging, though that might distract attention from the qualities of this typically excellent French liqueur, produced at the Abbey of Cenon, Bordeaux. Taking advantage of its perfect location between the **Cognac** and **Armagnac** areas, La Vieille Cure uses both brandies in which to macerate its 50 herbal ingredients. The green and yellow varieties have slightly different palates but the same alcohol content.

VIOLETTE, CRÈME DE (g) 25–40%

Liqueur made from the petals of violets, sometimes with additional flavor from **Curaçao** oranges.

VODKA (g) 35–80% •

A misunderstood and rather misrepresented term. In Slavic countries, vodka is a generic term for any spirit drink, whether it is distilled from grape, grain, potato, or whatever. The word is simply an ironic diminutive for water. In Poland and Russia these spirits are available in a wide variety of spiced and fruit versions, and even in the unflavored vodkas a degree of grain palate is sometimes deliberately retained, perhaps enhanced by aging. The most celebrated example of a delicately flavored vodka is Zubrowka, with a blade of grass in every bottle. The grass is of the type favored by the wild European bison, which graze on the borders of Poland and Russia. Of the unflavored vodkas, Tony Lord says in *The World Guide to Spirits*: "The bouquet of a clear Eastern vodka is spirity, with a light oiliness. ... the flavour is strong, spirity and almost 'green.'" It was nonetheless the early skill of the Slavs in producing very thoroughly distilled unflavored vodkas that inspired the idea of a neutral spirit as a basis for mixed drinks. The original purpose of this rectification was to produce a strong spirit that would not readily freeze in extreme weather. Alcohol freezes at a lower point than water. It was this rationale which produced the world's strongest commercially marketed liquor, Polish Pure Spirit (p) 80%. At a less ferocious level, the popularity of Smirnoff as a flag-carrier for neutral vodkas has compounded the dispute between the

Poles and Russians over the origins of that type of drink. If vodka is taken to mean a highly rectified and distilled neutral spirit with little or no flavor, as used in mixed drinks, where was it invented? Perhaps Smirnoff can provide the answer. Smirnoff originates from the city of Lvov, which has through most of its history been regarded as being Polish, but which is now in the Ukraine. Though they all look and taste much the same, "Western" vodkas are distilled from a wide variety of raw materials, ranging from beet in Turkey, and often molasses in Britain, to grain in the United States. Products which yield sugar distil very well, yet grain somehow has more respectability with the drinker; it really doesn't matter, and neutral vodka will always be distilled from what is available.

HARVEY WALLBANGER *DELICIOUS GALLIANO BLENDS BEAUTIFULLY WITH ORANGE JUICE IN THIS VERY SUMMERY COCKTAIL.* *SEE PAGE 180.*

WEISSE BIER (g) 2.5–3%

"White" beer, a term often applied when wheat is used in addition to the normal barley malt. These beers are often (but not always) very pale, and sometimes served unfiltered and hazy. The Berlin type is very low in alcohol, with the tartness of wheat greatly accentuated by a lactic fermentation. This beer is usually served with a dash of raspberry juice or green essence of woodruff. The Bavarian type, at a more conventional strength, is usually more wheaty, sometimes with fermentation characteristics that suggest bananas, plums, apples, or cloves. It is identified as Hefe-Weissbier if unfiltered; Kristall if bright; Dunkelweizen if dark; and Weizenbock if strong. The word *Weizen* means wheat.

WEIZENBIER (g) 5%

An alternative name for the above beer styles.

WHISKY, WHISKEY 40–60% •

Always spelled without the "e" in Scotland, and with it in the United States. Canada usually goes the Scottish way, and Ireland generally uses the "e." Each of the whisky-producing countries has its own style, for which it sets standards, but where does whisky begin and end? Consensus would seem to say that whisky is a spirit drink distilled from grain including a proportion of barley malt, which retains a pronounced flavor from its raw materials. This flavor may be heightened by the method of malting used (as in peaty Scotches) or by the type of cask used for aging. Whisky is an abbreviation and familiarization of *uisge*, and that of *uisge beatha* or *usquebaugh*, all being Gaelic for water of life. See **Bourbon**, **Irish whiskey**, **Rye**, and **Scotch**.

WHITE RUM (g) 40% •

Colorless rum of the light-bodied type produced in **Continuous stills**. See **Rum**.

WILD TURKEY (P)

Brand-name for robust **Bourbons**, at 43.4 and, famously, 50.5%. The name also appears on a smooth, sweetish **Rye**, and a whiskey-based liqueur that is honeyish and citric.

YVETTE, CRÈME (P)

Violet-petal liqueur made in honor of the French actress Yvette Gilbert at the turn of the century. The best-known liqueur of this type is made by Jacquin, of Philadelphia.

COCKTAILS

AND OTHER MIXED DRINKS

"A nicer discrimination ... refined taste ... the more genial customs which we have been led to adopt through our constant intercourse with France and other countries ... led to a beneficial change in our bibulous doings," says a charming work on mixed drinks produced in London around 1870.

That book clearly saw the claret cups of Bordeaux, ratafias of Savoy, and perhaps Piedmont's vermouths, which did much to modify rough gins of the day, to be the originals. It also recognized that the idea had already spread west in "those notions, many of which – owing to their racy character – are properly styled 'sensations' by our Yankee cousins."

A confusion of terms was employed to describe the various types of mixed drink: cobbler, cooler, crusta, cup, daisy, fix, flip, julep, negus, nog, sangaree, sling, smash, rickey, posset, punch. Most of these are still in use, and distinctions between them remain a matter of disagreement.

Another type of mixed drink described was "the cocktail – not so ancient an institution as juleps, etcetera, but with its next of kin 'crusta,' promises to maintain its ground." The typical recipe quoted specified bitters, ginger syrup, curaçao, and gin, stirred and served over ice in a tumbler, the rim of which had been moistened with lemon juice.

There are now about 10,000 mixed drinks recognized by the New York Bartenders' Guild, and there have been many more over the years, though the overwhelming majority are minor variations on a few great themes. Even the idea of a classic or standard mixed drink – of which any bartender can be expected to know – varies with fashion. In the list which follows, standard cocktails are marked ★.

There are almost as many explanations for the term cocktail, all

---

BLOODY MARY AND BLACK RUSSIAN *BOTH ARE VODKA-BASED, THE BLOODY MARY SERVING AS A FINE APERITIF AND A MORNING PICK-ME-UP.* *SEE PAGES 144–5.*

rather unlikely, and some decidedly tongue-in-cheek. Unable to leave Dr. Johnson out of it, the British enthusiast John Doxat attributes to him a contrived story about horses of mixed blood having cocked tails. In the American War of Independence, tavern-keeper Betsy Flanagan, widow of a Revolutionary soldier, is supposed to have stolen the tail feathers from a Tory neighbor's cock to decorate drinks. Several stories link mixed drinks with cockfighting lore: feathers were allegedly used to stir them for Mississippi gamblers, or was it British sailors, in the Gulf of Mexico? Then there was a story of the drink mixed by a beautiful Mexican girl called Coctel; surely that fits the spirit of the Tequila age?

It was the Jazz age that passed the cocktail into folk history, as a disguise for bootleg liquor, and Harry Craddock, the proponent of the Coctel story, who brought the mixing of drinks back across the Atlantic. His scholarly work at the Savoy Hotel in London elevated the serving of cocktails to the status of high art.

Although the word cocktail is often loosely used to describe all types of mixed drink, it does have a more specific meaning. The term cocktail is applied with precision to a short aperitif (and therefore a dry drink) based on a predominant hard spirit.

In such drinks, the base spirit should be tasted, and usually accounts for at least half the content. Some of the recipes which follow may be judged generous with hard liquor; they can always be scaled down as the evening goes on. In any event, a trial run is urged before anything new is offered to guests. About 12–16 mixed drinks should be obtainable from what British call simply a bottle and Americans a "fifth."

Brand-names of ingredients are given in the following list only where the originator of the recipe expressed a preference. Almost all liqueurs will considerably sweeten a drink, but many recipes call for further sugar in various forms. Although this is a matter of the originator's preference, sugar syrup dissolves the easiest. This can be made by simmering two cups of sugar in a pint of water. Once it has cooled down, the solution can be bottled and kept in the cocktail cabinet or bar. The sweeter drinks are singled out with the symbol ♥.

Truly short drinks are identified 🍸; anything longer is marked ▮.

For the best chilling, put the ice in first. To avoid waste and keep tabs on what drinks you are mixing, put the base spirit in last. Craftily spray soda into the ice bucket to keep the cubes separate, warm in advance anything that is to be flambéed, and have a good time.

ABERDEEN ANGUS

2 oz. Scotch whisky,
1 oz. Drambuie,
1 tablespoon honey,
2 tablespoons lime juice
Stir the Scotch, honey, and lime juice in a drinking mug until they are blended. Warm the Drambuie in a ladle over a low flame. Ignite it, and pour the burning liqueur into the mug. Stir vigorously, and drink immediately from the mug.

Restores the energy after a strenuous few hours on the grouse moors. Although Scotch whisky has too delicate a palate to work well in many mixed drinks, this one was made for it. Single malt seems a sinful extravagance in a mixed drink anyway, and a Highland might be more geographically appropriate, but a really peaty Islay makes for a truly distinctive drink.

ABSINTHE SUISSESSE ♥

1½ oz. Pernod or other anis,
2 or 3 drops anisette,
2 or 3 drops orange-flower water,
modest teaspoon white crème de menthe or peppermint schnapps,
1 egg white
Shake with ice, and strain into a cocktail glass.

For absinthe, substitute Pernod. Both, of course, originated in Switzerland. Non-Gallic drinkers sometimes find Pernod a little heavy, and it is lightened delightfully in this pre- or post-prandial cocktail, which was probably invented not in Europe but in Louisiana.

ACAPULCO ♥

1½ oz. tequila,
1½ oz. Jamaica rum,
3 oz. pineapple juice,
1 oz. (or slightly less) grapefruit or lime juice,
cubes of fresh pineapple (optional)
Shake with ice cubes, and serve on the rocks in a Collins glass, garnished with the pineapple.

A potent and robust restorative after the pleasures of a hot day. This tequila version seems most appropriate, although another recipe employs *triple sec* and uses the white of an egg.

ADMIRAL

1 oz. bourbon,
2 oz. dry vermouth,
juice of ½ lemon, twist of peel
Shake well with ice. Serve on the rocks in an Old Fashioned glass, decorated with the twist of lemon.

Jazz-lovers may respond best to Benny Goodman's version of this old standard, but uncharacteristically he was heavy-handed when it came to vermouth.

ADONIS

2 oz. dry sherry,
1 oz. sweet Italian vermouth,
2 dashes of Angostura bitters
Stir well with ice, and strain into a cocktail glass.

A classic cocktail which is a splendid aperitif. Some bartenders prefer to use orange bitters.

AFFINITY

★ ♥

½ oz. dry French vermouth,
½ oz. sweet Italian vermouth,
¼ oz. crème de violette
Shake with ice, and strain into a cocktail glass.

The traditional recipe, as set out in *The Savoy Cocktail Book*, uses Scotch whisky with equal parts of dry and sweet vermouth, and dashes of Angostura bitters. Trader Vic's version, given here, is more fun.

AKVAVIT CLAM

3 oz. Danish akvavit,
1½ oz. clam juice,
1½ oz. tomato juice,
1 teaspoon lemon juice,
½ teaspoon Worcestershire sauce, pinch of salt, black pepper, and cayenne pepper
Stir vigorously in a mixing glass and chill. Serve with ice in an Old Fashioned glass.

One of those aperitifs which feeds the drinker while at the same time rousing his appetite to further challenges.

ALASKA

★

2 oz. (or even more) London Dry gin,
½ oz. (or even less) green Chartreuse,
½ oz. dry sherry (optional),
twist of lemon peel
Stir thoroughly with ice cubes, and strain into a cocktail glass. Decorate with the lemon peel.

An excuse to get out the Chartreuse for a good old glamorous cocktail before dinner or the theater. Opinions vary over the quantities, but too much Chartreuse makes for a sweet drink.

ALASKA *A SOPHISTICATED COCKTAIL WITH CHARTREUSE, THE FRENCH LIQUEUR MADE FROM A SECRET RECIPE USING 130 HERBS, BRANDY, AND MOUNTAIN HONEY.*

ALCUDIA

2 oz. dry gin,
1 oz. Galliano,
1 oz. crème de banane,
1 oz. grapefruit juice,
twist of grapefruit peel

Shake with ice cubes, and strain into a cocktail glass. Decorate with the twist.

Galliano has featured in many cocktails since it was popularized by being used in the **Harvey Wallbanger**. This example is teasingly sweet and dry.

ALE FLIP

1 quart ale,
2 egg whites, 4 egg yolks,
4 tablespoons sugar,
nutmeg

Bring the ale gently to a boil in a saucepan. Beat the egg whites until they are frothy. Beat the yolks, and mix with the whites and the sugar. Pour the mixture very slowly into the beer, stirring vigorously. Pour the beer to and fro between two pans several times to create a frothy head. Serve in heat-proof mugs, with a dusting of nutmeg.

Can be drunk chilled, but is better as a hot drink. Best with a bitter but full-bodied British brew, although good results have been obtained with American ales such as Rainier, from Seattle, or even with Anchor Steam Beer. Serves four.

ALEXANDER see **Brandy Alexander**

ALFONSO COCKTAIL ★

2 tablespoons Dubonnet,
dash of Angostura or Péychaud bitters,
1 lump sugar,
champagne,
twist of lemon peel

Put the sugar in a large, saucer-shaped champagne glass, and sprinkle with bitters. Add the Dubonnet and an ice cube, then fill with well-chilled champagne, and decorate with the twist.

For those blasé folk who genuinely feel that neat champagne is rather boring.

ALFONSO SPECIAL ★

1½ oz. Grand Marnier,
¾ oz. dry gin,
¾ oz. dry vermouth,
4 dashes of sweet vermouth,
dash of Angostura bitters
Stir well with ice, and strain into a cocktail glass.

The Grand Marnier makes this an interesting sweet-and-dry experience.

ALGONQUIN

2 oz. rye,
1 oz. dry vermouth,
1 oz. pineapple juice
Shake with ice, and serve on the rocks in an Old Fashioned glass.

A cocktail to inspire literary witticisms. Wouldn't Dorothy Parker have agreed that liquor is quicker?

ALL-WHITE FRAPPÉ ♥

1 oz. peppermint schnapps,
1 oz. white crème de cacao,
1 oz. anisette,
1 oz. lemon juice
Shake with ice cubes, and strain over crushed ice in a cocktail glass.

Virginally pretty, and rather sweet, especially if crème de menthe is preferred.

ALTERED STATES see Pousse-café

AMARETTO HEARTWARMER

2 oz. Southern Comfort,
1 oz. dry vermouth,
1 oz. Amaretto,
2 blanched almonds,
1 crushed peach kernel,
½ teaspoon sugar
Warm the Southern Comfort. Add the almonds, kernel, and sugar, and stir. Allow to cool. Add the Amaretto, and stir. Strain over lots of ice in an Old Fashioned glass.

This recipe is a version of the Almond Cocktail.

AMBASSADOR

2 oz. tequila,
fresh orange juice to taste,
1 teaspoon sugar syrup,
slice of orange
Stir. Serve on the rocks in an Old Fashioned or Collins glass, garnished with the orange slice.

Barely a cocktail, but a simple and effective refresher.

AMER PICON COCKTAIL

¾ oz. Amer Picon,
¾ oz. sweet Italian vermouth,
Shake with ice cubes, and strain into a chilled cocktail glass.

Several delicious aperitifs are served under this name. In one version the Amer Picon is simply laced with a teaspoon of grenadine and Perrier is added to taste. In another, the juice of a lime is added to this mixture. Trader Vic's recipe comes with a guarantee that it will arouse hunger.

AMERICAN BEAUTY

★ ♥

¾ oz. brandy,
¾ oz. dry vermouth,
¾ oz. orange juice,
¼ oz. white crème de menthe or peppermint schnapps,
dash of grenadine,
1 oz. port
Shake all the ingredients except the port with crushed ice. Strain into an Old Fashioned or cocktail glass. Tilt the glass, and slowly add the port so that it floats on top.

All things nice are in this classic cocktail. Perhaps that is why, when imbibed in moderation, it settles both the stomach and the mind.

AMERICANO

★

¾ oz. Campari,
¾ oz. Italian sweet vermouth,
soda to taste,
slice of orange
Stir well in an Old Fashioned glass generously loaded with ice cubes. Garnish with the orange slice.

An Italiano, really. One of those sunny aperitifs that is also very refreshing. May also be made in a very large ballon wine glass.

AMERICANO *A 'SPIRIT-FREE' BUT NONETHELESS ALCOHOLIC COCKTAIL BASED ON VERMOUTH.*

APERITIF PERRIER

1½ oz. London Dry gin,
1½ oz. Noilly Prat,
½ oz. Rose's lime juice (or 3 oz. fresh lime or grapefruit juice),
Perrier,
twist of cucumber peel

Shake the liquor and fruit juice very thoroughly with ice cubes, and strain into a ballon wine glass, or Collins glass, over 2 or 3 ice cubes. Top up with Perrier and decorate with the cucumber peel.

Converts a hard day at the top into a healthy appetite. Long before America discovered Perrier it was a favorite in Europe, not only for its natural sparkle but also for its stomach-settling qualities. Purists may object to the addition of alcohol, but Perrier was made famous by an Englishman, A. W. St.-John Harmsworth, so it should go well with London Dry and French.

APPLE TODDY

1 cooking apple,
1 bottle apple brandy,
1½ oz. grape or other fruit brandy according to taste,
4 lemon slices stuck with cloves,
1 stick cinnamon,
1 tablespoon sugar

Bake the apple and remove the skin. In each of 4 heat-proof glasses, place a quarter of the apple pulp, a sprinkling of sugar, a slice of lemon, and a piece of cinnamon. Pour on the brandy. Top up with boiling water, and stir.

For autumn evenings. Tastes better if the apple is marinated in the brandy for two or three days, but this is not essential.

APPLEJACK PUNCH

2 bottles applejack,
1 pint lemon juice,
1 pint orange juice,
6 oz. grenadine,
2 large bottles ginger ale,
apple slices,
mint sprigs

Stir all ingredients except the ginger ale vigorously with lots of chunky ice in a punch bowl. Add ginger ale just before serving. Decorate with the apple slices and mint sprigs.

Many recipes. This one will serve a couple of dozen experienced drinkers.

APPLEJACK RABBIT

★

1½ oz. apple brandy,
½ oz. lemon juice,
½ oz. lime or orange juice, according to taste,
½ teaspoon maple syrup
Shake thoroughly with ice. Dip the rim of an Old Fashioned glass in maple syrup, and line it with sugar. Strain the Rabbit into the glass over lots of ice.

There are applejack cocktails made with curaçao or sweet vermouth, and there is the Rabbit, which is both decorative and tasty.

ATHOLL BROSE

1½ oz. Scotch whisky,
1½ oz. clear honey,
1½ oz. heavy cream
Mix well in a warm glass or ramekin dish. Allow to cool, and chill.

Not so much the original oatmeal drink as an extremely Scottish dessert which has attained a certain chic in English dining circles.

AZTEC PUNCH

1 gallon tequila,
5 gallons grapefruit juice,
2 quarts dark tea,
3 cups lemon juice,
1 cup sugar syrup
Stir together in a punch bowl, with large blocks of ice.

Tequila packs the punch, of course. Serves about 20.

BACARDI SPECIAL

★

2 oz. Bacardi rum,
¾ oz. gin,
juice of 1 small lime,
dash of grenadine,
½ teaspoon sugar
Shake all the ingredients except the rum with cracked ice until cold. Add the rum, shake again until cold. Strain into a cocktail glass.

The best known among the several cocktails that insist on the Bacardi brand. A **Daiquiri** variation.

BALTIMORE EGG NOG

There are numerous recipes for this party standby.

1 oz. cognac or other brandy,
1½ oz. madeira,
½ oz. Jamaica rum,
2 teaspoons sugar syrup,
1 egg,
4 oz. fresh milk,
2 oz. heavy cream

Shake vigorously with ice cubes. Strain into a Collins glass. Top up with cold milk, and dust with grated nutmeg, if liked.

BANANA BIRD

Lovers of the fruit itself may have more fun in the **Daiquiri** department, but the Banana Bird is an interesting, if unpretentious, cocktail.

1 oz. bourbon,
2 teaspoons crème de banane,
***2 teaspoons* triple sec**
(Cointreau is a good example),
1 oz. heavy cream

Shake with ice, and strain into a cocktail glass.

BEER SANGAREE

A simpler drink than a flip, a mixed drink consisting of a sweetened spiced liquor to which eggs have been added. Sangarees are more commonly made with wine.

½ pint strong ale or porter,
1–2 teaspoons sugar syrup or sugar,
nutmeg

Lightly chill the beer. Place the sugar in a Collins glass, add a little water, stir, pour on the beer and dust with grated nutmeg.

BELLINI

From Harry's Bar in Venice, this was a film-crowd favorite in the "swinging sixties." For lazy afternoons and beautiful people. Serves four.

1 bottle champagne,
3 or 4 peaches,
sprinkling of sugar

Purée the peaches and sugar, thoroughly chill the champagne and stir together gently in a punch bowl until blended. Decant into elegant glasses.

BERMUDA ROSE

There is also the Bouquet, but the single Rose is the best-known Bermuda cocktail.

1½ oz. gin,
1 tablespoon lime juice,
2 or 3 drops each of apricot brandy and grenadine

Shake with ice cubes, and strain over ice into an Old Fashioned glass.

BETSY ROSS

★ 🍸

1½ oz. brandy,
1 oz. port,
1 teaspoon Cointreau,
dash of Angostura bitters
Shake with ice cubes, and strain into an Old Fashioned glass, with ice cubes.

Revives the spirit and settles the stomach. Some argue that the brandy should be Spanish, and in much greater quantity.

BETWEEN THE SHEETS

★ 🍸

1 oz. Cointreau,
1 oz. brandy,
1 oz. white rum,
1 oz. lime juice (optional),
twist of lemon peel
Shake with cracked ice, strain into a saucer-shaped champagne glass, and decorate with the lemon peel.

One of the classics, despite its rather vulgar name.

BIG APPLE

1 eating apple,
3 oz. apple brandy,
2 oz. orange juice,
1 oz. lemon juice
Cut a hole in the top of the apple and scoop out the core and enough of the pulp to make plenty of room for the drink. Place the apple shell in the ice compartment of the refrigerator for about 15 minutes. Mix the rest of the ingredients very thoroughly with the apple pulp in a blender. Strain into the apple shell, and serve with a straw – or two.

You drink out of the apple in the most colorful version of this summery "I love New York" potion.

THE BIG APPLE A COCKTAIL FOR SHARING

THE BISHOP

1 large orange,
12 cloves,
1 quart inexpensive port,
1 tablespoon honey,
1 teaspoon allspice (optional),
a few dashes of cognac

Stud the orange with the cloves, and bake it at a low temperature for about 30 minutes. Cut the baked orange into quarters, and put in a pan with the remaining ingredients. Simmer over a very low flame for 20 minutes. Do not boil. Serve in heated cups.

A wine drink made with baked orange, and usually served hot. Variations include The Cardinal (claret) and The Pope (champagne). This one is called The English Bishop. Serves six.

BLACK RUSSIAN ★

1½ oz. vodka
¾ oz. Kahlúa or Tia Maria

Shake with ice, and strain into a cocktail glass.

A stylish after-dinner cocktail which may be made less sweet by adding a drop or two of lemon juice, in which case it becomes a Black Magic. For those unsociable enough to smoke after dinner, a Sobranie cigarette would be appropriate.

BLACK VELVET

Equal parts of champagne or good sparkling wine (must be very dry) and Bitter Stout (Guinness, Murphy, Beamish)

Chill all the ingredients, then pour them simultaneously into a large pitcher, and decant into the tallest glasses you can find.

The most delicious Gaelic–Gallic conspiracy since Wolfe Tone's rather more political essay. Wonderful for an outdoor party on a summer's afternoon.

BLACKTHORN, ENGLISH

1 oz. sloe gin,
1 oz. (or less) Italian sweet vermouth,
1 oz. Plymouth gin (optional),
2 dashes orange bitters

Stir with ice, and strain into a cocktail glass.

Being the fruit of the blackthorn, surely the sloe should flavor this cocktail? Sloe gin may be half-forgotten, but it does have a wistful English charm.

BLACKTHORN, IRISH

1½ oz. Irish whiskey,
1½ oz. dry vermouth,
3 dashes of Pernod,
3 dashes of Angostura bitters
Stir with ice cubes, and serve on the rocks in an Old Fashioned glass.

To be sure, isn't a blackthorn a shillelagh, and therefore a Hibernian invention?

BLENDED COMFORT

1 oz. Southern Comfort,
2 oz. bourbon,
½ oz. dry vermouth,
1 oz. orange juice,
2 tablespoons lemon juice,
4 oz. crushed ice,
¼ peach and slice of peach, plus slice of orange
Skin the peach quarter. Mix the ingredients in a blender at low speed for 10 to 15 seconds. Strain over crushed ice in a Collins glass. Decorate with the peach slice and orange slice.

One of many excellent mixed drinks made with Southern Comfort.

BLOODY MARY ★

1½ oz. vodka,
1 small tin tomato juice (about 3 oz.),
1 oz. lemon juice,
1 barspoon Worcestershire sauce,
2 drops of Tabasco (optional),
salt and pepper,
slice of lemon (optional)
Shake with 3 ice cubes and strain into an Old Fashioned glass, or a ballon wine glass, with salt and pepper to taste. If you like, decorate with a slice of lemon.

Surely the drink that did the most to popularize the Western version of vodka, notwithstanding the inevitable later variations using other spirits. Everyone has an opinion on the Bloody Mary. In *The Fine Art of Mixing Drinks*, David Embury describes it as "a classic example of combining in one potion both the poison and the antidote." Gourmet and restaurateur Robert Carrier adds sherry and celery salt. Blender freaks have even been known to use celery leaves and the white of an egg. It depends whether you want a drink or a meal.

BLUE BLAZER ★ 🍸

A truly spectacular and extremely difficult – not to mention dangerous – drink to serve.

1 teaspoon or more sugar (or 1 tablespoon honey),
4 oz. warmed Scotch,
twist of lemon peel or grated nutmeg

Warm two ½-pint metal tankards or mugs. In one, dissolve the sugar or honey in about 3 oz. boiling water. Pour the Scotch into the other and light it. While it blazes, pour the Scotch back and forth from one mug to the other, to create a continuous stream of fire. When the flame dies down, pour the liquid into a heated wine glass. Decorate with lemon, or dust with nutmeg.

BLUE HAWAIIAN ♥ 🍸

A colorful concoction which causes geographical confusion by coming from the Zanzibar Club, London. An after-office drink for smart young things.

½ oz. blue curaçao,
2 oz. Bacardi,
1 oz. pineapple juice,
1 teaspoon coconut cream

Shake with ice cubes, and strain into a cocktail glass.

BOLO see English Bolo

BOSOM CARESSER ★ 🍸

Warming and sweet, this is for tender moments only.

½ oz. madeira,
¼ oz. brandy,
¼ oz. curaçao,
1 teaspoon grenadine,
1 egg yolk

Shake with ice, and strain into a cocktail glass.

BOSTON COCKTAIL 🍸

A civilized New England aperitif.

1½ oz. dry gin,
1 oz. apricot brandy,
1 teaspoon lemon juice,
dash of grenadine

Shake with ice, and strain into a cocktail glass.

BOURBON COCKTAIL

2 oz. bourbon,
1 oz. lemon juice,
⅓ oz. curaçao,
⅓ oz. Benedictine,
dash of Angostura bitters
Shake with cracked ice, and strain into a cocktail glass, or serve on the rocks in an Old Fashioned glass, decorated with a twist of lemon.

Because of their sweet and fuller palate, American whiskeys are happier in cocktails than their sensitive European cousins, but they are not natural mixers. They marry best with flavors like peach and orange. This recipe is based loosely on David Embury's ideal bourbon cocktail.

BOURBON FOG

1 pint bourbon,
1 pint well-chilled, very strong black coffee,
1 pint vanilla ice cream
Mix thoroughly in a punch bowl, and serve with a little ice in Old Fashioned or Collins glasses.

Although today there are few foggy days in London Town, that is where this recipe came from, by the hand of John Doxat, a drinker of great distinction. In fact, it should clear the fog for all but the most misty late-night reveller. Serves 15 to 20.

BRANDIED GINGER

1 oz. brandy,
½ oz. ginger brandy or ginger wine,
1 teaspoon (or more) lime juice,
1 teaspoon orange juice,
1 piece preserved ginger and/or grated chocolate
Shake with ice cubes, strain into a cocktail glass, and decorate with the ginger, and/or dust with the chocolate.

A delicious combination of treats for midafternoon or after dinner.

BRANDY ALEXANDER

★ ♥

1½ oz. cognac or armagnac,
1 oz. dark crème de cacao,
1 oz. heavy cream,
nutmeg
Shake well with ice cubes, strain into a cocktail glass, and dust with nutmeg.

An extravagant cocktail for an afternoon rendezvous. It is as toothsome as candy, but as seductive as surreptitious liquor.

BRAVE BULL

1 oz. tequila,
1½ oz. Kahlúa or Tia Maria
Stir and pour over ice in an Old Fashioned glass.

Although its ingredients are from the Americas, this is a British recipe.

BRONX

★

1½ oz. gin,
½ oz. dry vermouth,
½ oz. (or less) sweet vermouth,
½ oz. orange juice,
½ oz. lemon juice (optional)
Shake very briskly with ice cubes, strain into a wine glass, or serve on the rocks in an Old Fashioned glass.

Probably one of the many cocktails that were devised to disguise bootlegging from both the police and the palate during Prohibition. For a truly dry aperitif cocktail, forget the sweet vermouth. Use a blood orange for a Bloody Bronx; add an egg yolk for a sickly Golden Bronx.

THE BUCK

★

1½ oz. brandy,
1 oz. lemon juice,
¾ oz. crème de menthe,
ginger ale,
a few seedless grapes
Shake all the ingredients except the ginger ale with cracked ice. Serve on the rocks in a Collins glass, top up with ginger ale, stir with a barspoon, and decorate with the grapes.

Another product of Prohibition, in which the distinguishing feature was the use of ginger and lemon juice. A quarter of the lemon was actually used as garnish. The original Buck was made with gin, like so many of the traditional mixed drinks. While there is in most instances a strong case for maintaining that tradition, there is also much to be said for this unusual Brandy Buck recipe. Why should gin have all the fun?

BUCK'S FIZZ

★

1 bottle chilled champagne,
8 oz. fresh orange juice
Pour the orange juice into a pitcher, then add the champagne. Decant into large, tall glasses.

Neither a Buck nor a Fizz in the gin sense, but a long, refreshing drink in which champagne provides the uplift while the goodness of fresh orange juice cushions any subsequent letdown. Regency bucks knew what they were doing. Serves four to six.

BUCK'S FIZZ contd.

Mimosa is a prettier name for a Buck's Fizz. Make a difference by adding ½ oz. of Cointreau to each drink.

BULLSHOT

2 oz. vodka,
4 oz. beef bouillon or 1 small can condensed consommé,
1 barspoon Worcestershire sauce,
dash of Tabasco (optional),
dash of cayenne pepper,
salt to taste,
juice of ½ a lemon,
slice of lemon

Stir vigorously with plenty of ice, and strain into an Old Fashioned glass, with a cube of ice and the lemon slice.

Authorities differ on the uses of this clever and nutritious mixed drink. Trader Vic says it is a good way to keep warm at a cold ballgame; John Doxat recommends it for breakfast on the morning after; everyone agrees that it is a relatively palatable "hair of the dog."

BURGUNDY COCKTAIL

3 oz. red burgundy,
1 oz. cognac,
3–4 drops maraschino,
slice of lemon or 1 cherry

Stir with ice cubes, strain into a cocktail glass, and decorate with the lemon slice or cherry.

The only recognized cocktail to use red burgundy as its basic ingredient. Warming and sweet after-dinner drink.

BYRRH COCKTAIL

½ oz. rye,
½ oz. Byrrh,
½ oz. dry French vermouth

Shake with ice, and strain into a cocktail glass.

Despite the fact that it is pronounced rather like "beer," the drink which gives its name to this cocktail is a typically French aperitif. A measure of Byrrh goes nicely with a slightly smaller quantity of crème de cassis, ice, and soda, but bartenders like to marry it with a hard liquor, whether gin, bourbon, or rye. The latter works best.

CAFÉ AMARETTO

½ oz. Amaretto,
½ oz. Kahlúa (or Tia Maria) or quantities to taste,
1 cup scalding hot coffee,
whipped cream

Pour the liqueurs into the coffee and top with the whipped cream.

A simple but delicious rich coffee from the Souper, Aspen, Colorado. They call it Souper Coffee. Serve with Amaretti biscuits.

CAFÉ BRÛLOT

8 oz. cognac,
1 pint scalding hot coffee,
2 sugar cubes,
the peel of 1 lemon and 1 orange cut in a spiral,
8 cloves,
1 chopped vanilla bean,
2–3 sticks cinnamon

Pour the brandy into a bowl, preferably made of silver. Add one sugar cube, the cloves, vanilla, cinnamon, orange and lemon peel. Stir well. Pour in the coffee. Soak the remaining cube of sugar in cognac, place it on a spoon, and light it. Dip the spoon containing the blazing cube into the coffee mixture, so that the flame spreads across the surface. Serve in small coffee cups.

There are many flaming coffees with a variety of colorful names, and quite a few just called Café Brûlot. It is possible simply to float an ounce of cognac on top of a glass of hot coffee, and flame the liquor to great effect. The basic Brûlot is more of a punch, and this recipe can be embellished and varied to taste. Serves eight.

CALISAY COCKTAIL ♥

1 oz. Calisay,
1 oz. sweet Italian vermouth,
3 dashes of sugar syrup,
3 dashes of lime juice

Shake well with ice cubes, and strain into a cocktail glass.

The excellent but slightly syrupy quinine liqueur of Catalonia is seldom used in cocktails. This rare example is rather sweet, and can be given more after-dinner appeal with a slug of Spanish brandy.

CANADIAN SUNSET

2 oz. Canadian whisky,
1 oz. Galliano,
1 oz. Strega,
2 oz. lemon juice,
2 dashes of Angostura bitters,
1 barspoon of grenadine
Place the grenadine in a cocktail glass. Shake the remaining ingredients with ice cubes, and strain over the grenadine.

Until this modern cocktail was devised, Canada lent its name only to a rather inappropriate rum-based drink and a northern variation of the Old Fashioned.

CAPE CODDER

2 oz. vodka,
juice of ½ lime,
4 oz. cranberry juice
Shake with ice, and serve on the rocks in a Collins glass.

This sustaining and refreshing drink may be varied by the use of light rum or applejack as its base, and by the addition of soda.

CARABINIERI

¾ oz. Galliano,
1 oz. tequila,
½ oz. Cointreau,
1 teaspoon Rose's lime juice,
1 egg yolk,
slice of lime,
1 green and 1 red cherry
Shake thoroughly, and strain into a Collins glass over crushed ice. Garnish with the lime slice and cherries.

A cosmopolitan Canadian cocktail, from Francisco Pedroche, of the Hyatt Regency Hotel, Toronto.

CARIBBEAN CHAMPAGNE

4 oz. dry champagne,
½ teaspoon white rum,
½ teaspoon crème de banane,
1–2 dashes of orange bitters,
1 slice banana
Stir with crushed ice in a saucer-shaped champagne glass. Decorate with the banana slice.

This one is a delicious sweet-and-dry extravagance.

CASABLANCA

Bogey never sampled this recipe from Japan, but it provides a rare opportunity to make good use of advocaat.

1 oz. vodka,
½ oz. (or fractionally more) advocaat,
1 teaspoon (or fractionally more) Galliano,
1 tablespoon lemon juice,
1 teaspoon orange juice

Shake and serve over crushed ice in a cocktail glass, decorated with a thin slice of orange.

CHABLIS CUP

An unusual refresher. Serves four.

1 bottle Chablis,
4 oz. Grand Marnier,
4 oz. kirsch,
2 to 3 peaches,
1 orange,
cherries,
3 tablespoons powdered sugar,
mint sprigs

Peel and cut up the peaches, reserving any juice. Slice the orange, and place with the cherries in a small punch bowl. Pour on the Chablis, and add the powdered sugar. Stir gently, and refrigerate for about 30 minutes. Garnish with sprigs of mint, and serve in wine glasses.

CHERRY BLOSSOM

★ ♥

Unquestionably a standard cocktail, and it comes in two versions, yet neither works very well. Trader Vic says rather harshly "take your pick; they're both lousy." One version has nothing to do with cherries; it is made with gin, raspberry syrup, orange bitters, and egg white. This is the other version.

1 oz. cherry brandy,
1 oz. cognac,
a few drops of grenadine,
a few drops of curaçao,
½ oz. lemon juice,
sugar (optional)

Shake very thoroughly with ice cubes (the drink should be very cold), and strain into a cocktail glass which has been sugar-rimmed with cherry brandy.

CHICAGO BOMB ♥ 🍸

2 oz. vanilla ice cream,
1 teaspoon white crème de cacao,
1 teaspoon green crème de menthe

Mix with cracked ice in an electric blender for a few seconds at high speed. Serve straight up in a cocktail glass.

The city's own drink should surely be made with bouillon. Instead, Chicago offers the choice of a rum fizz, a sort of champagne cocktail, and this rather sickly bomb.

CHINESE COCKTAIL ★ ♥ 🍸

1½ oz. Jamaica rum,
1 tablespoon grenadine,
a few dashes of curaçao,
a few dashes of maraschino,
1–2 dashes of Angostura bitters

Shake with cracked ice, and strain into a cocktail glass.

Perhaps the rediscovery of China will lead us to a truly oriental cocktail. Until that happens, the best thing to drink before, during, and after a Chinese meal is probably either tea or heated sake. The classic Chinese Cocktail has little to do with the East.

CHOCOLATE COCKTAIL ♥ 🍸

1 teaspoon grated dark chocolate,
1 egg yolk,
2 oz. yellow Chartreuse,
1½ oz. port

Shake thoroughly, and strain into a cocktail or wine glass.

A most unusual recipe from Harry Craddock, the godfather of all bartenders.

CIDER CUP

1 quart dry cider,
3 tablespoons brandy,
3 tablespoons Cointreau and/or maraschino,
juice of 1 lemon,
½ pint fresh orange juice and/or soda,
orange and lemon slices

Thoroughly chill the cider. Mix it with the remaining ingredients in a punch bowl, adding the orange and lemon slices and ice at the last minute. Serve in wine glasses.

The West of England ciders are ferocious enough to knock a man legless. Away from their homeland, however, they are only found in a tame condition which makes them fun at a party, in punches, possets (hot, milky drinks), and syllabubs (creamy desserts). Serves four.

THE CLARIDGE ★

1 oz. London Dry gin,
1 oz. French dry vermouth,
½ oz. Cointreau,
½ oz. apricot brandy
Shake well with ice cubes, and strain into a cocktail glass.

An elegant early evening drink. It does not matter whether you're in London staying at Claridges or just putting on the Ritz. Recipe from *The Savoy Cocktail Book*.

CLOVER CLUB ★

1½ oz. London Dry gin,
½ oz. grenadine,
juice of ½ lime,
1 egg white
Shake well with ice cubes, and strain into a cocktail glass.

An early classic which remains popular, and tops the list at Harry's Bar in the Park Lane Hotel, London.

THE COBBLER ♥

1 teaspoon sugar syrup,
dash of grenadine,
dash of curaçao,
3 oz. medium dry sherry
The ingredients are neither stirred nor shaken before being poured into a large wine glass over crushed ice. Pour sugar or fruit syrup over the ice first, then the curaçao, then the sherry. Stir with a barspoon, churning the ice until the drink has a frosted appearance. A Cobbler is usually decorated with seasonal fruits and served with straws.

A style of mixed drink which is at least a century old. Cobblers are often made with wine (claret, Rhine wines, Sauternes, or fortified wine) instead of spirit as a base. The original may well be the Sherry Cobbler.

COCONUT SHELL ♥

3 oz. light or golden rum,
1½ oz. crème de banane,
2 large fresh coconuts
Drain the coconuts, reserving the liquid. Scoop out the flesh, and mix it with the milk and other ingredients, with 3–4 oz. crushed ice. Blend at high speed. If it is insufficiently liquid, add a little cream. Serve in the coconut shells.

Part of the fun comes from drinking out of the shell, of course, although coconut water is both delicious and nutritious. There are lots of coconut drinks, usually based on rum, but occasionally on brandy, or even bourbon. Complementary flavors include maraschino, almond, and grapefruit.

COCONUT TEQUILA

A sweet and happy marriage.

1½ oz. tequila,
2 teaspoons lemon juice,
2 teaspoons cream of coconut,
1 teaspoon maraschino

Mix in a blender at low speed for 15 seconds, with crushed ice. Strain into a cocktail glass.

COFFEE see Café

COCONUT SHELL *A REFRESHING BLEND OF CARIBBEAN FLAVORS FOR SHARING ON LAZY DAYS IN SUMMER.*

THE COLLINS ★

3 oz. gin,
juice of 1 large lemon,
1 tablespoon (or less) sugar syrup,
soda

Pour ingredients into the tallest Collins glass you can find, add five large ice cubes and top up with soda. Stir thoroughly.

A rhyme from the 1890s refers to a John Collins who was a London bartender. At that time, much of the gin produced there was still of the original Dutch type, which might explain why a John Collins was originally made with Hollands. The derivation of the Tom Collins may be just as simple: this version was originally made with sweetened gin, the best-known brand of which was Old Tom. Although Hollands gin is still readily available, and Old Tom continues to be produced in limited quantities, the two Collins are both commonly made with dry gin, and their names have become hopelessly confused. They have also been joined by Mike Collins (Irish whiskey), Jack (apple brandy) and such unlikely cousins as Pierre (cognac) and Pedro (rum). No doubt Juan (tequila) is lurking round the corner. A Collins is made with spirit, lemon and sugar. It is distinguished most of all from **The Sour** by its size. A Collins is the tallest of mixed drinks, and is intended to be as refreshing as a lemonade, but with an added kick.

COOCH BEHAR

1½ oz. pepper vodka,
3 oz. tomato juice

Shake thoroughly, and serve on the rocks in an Old Fashioned glass.

An Indian recipe devised by a maharajah of Cooch Behar. If you cannot find pepper vodka (Okhotnichya is a Russian brand), make your own. Steep a hot Mexican or Italian pepper in regular vodka for as long as you can wait, preferably for a few weeks.

THE COOLER

1½ oz. dry gin,
1½ oz. apricot brandy (liqueur),
juice of 1 lemon,
2 dashes of grenadine,
soda,
2 or 3 fresh sprigs of mint
Prepare as for the Collins. Decorate with the mint.

A term rather vaguely used for other long, iced mixed drinks served in Collins glasses. A Cooler is dry, and may contain a couple of dashes of grenadine and a dash of bitters. Ginger ale may be used instead of soda. The ice may be cracked. David Embury decorates his Coolers with the peel of a whole lemon or orange, cut in a continuous spiral, curling over the edge of the glass, as in a **Horse's Neck**. This is the Sea Breeze Cooler.

CORPSE REVIVER

1. 1 oz. cognac,
1 oz. Fernet Branca,
1 oz. white crème de menthe or peppermint schnapps
2. 2 oz. cognac,
1 oz. calvados or applejack,
1 oz. sweet Italian vermouth
3. 1 oz. dry gin,
1 oz. Cointreau,
1 oz. China-Martini or Swedish punsch,
1 oz. lemon juice,
dash of Pernod
In each case retire to a soundproof room while someone else shakes the mixture very thoroughly before straining into a cocktail glass.

The name has clearly caught the imagination of many bartenders, for there are at least three well-established varieties of Corpse Reviver, each one intended to be a well-bred hair of the dog. Endless variations, not to mention Sally Bowles' toothpaste "oyster."

THE CRUSTA

2 oz. brandy,
½ oz. lemon juice,
1 teaspoon maraschino,
1 teaspoon curaçao (optional),
2 dashes of bitters,
peel of 1 lemon (or orange), cut in a continuous spiral

Line glass with the peel. Moisten the edge of the glass, and dip in sugar, to frost the rim and the upper edge of the peel. Shake ingredients with crushed ice, and strain into the glass.

An elaborate version of **The Sour**, best served in a wine glass, and most often made with brandy.

CUBA LIBRE

★

1 lime,
2 oz. Bacardi or other light rum,
Coca-Cola

Squeeze the lime into a Collins glass, and drop in the lime shells. Pound them with a barspoon. Fill the glass with large ice cubes. Add rum, then top up with Coke. Stir lightly but thoroughly.

It is not quite clear who liberated what from whom, except that the Bacardi company left Cuba for Puerto Rico. After all their efforts, one authority recommends Philippine rum, which hardly seems appropriate. A miniature version is sometimes made for the cocktail glass, and the whole thing can be reformulated with Southern Comfort.

THE CUP

3 glasses marsala or madeira,
1 bottle inexpensive white wine,
½ a lemon,
1 pint (or more) soda,
borage

Slice the lemon, and mix with all ingredients except soda, in a jug or bowl, with chunks of ice. Refrigerate for at least 2 hours. Add soda just before serving; stir gently. The borage leaf adds an agreeable cucumberish flavor to summer cups; the flower makes a pleasant floating decoration.

A wine-based summer drink mixed in quantity. See **Cider Cup** and **Chablis Cup**. The Coronation Crystal Cup is unusual in that it employs marsala, a fortified wine often confined to the kitchen. Serves four to six.

CRUSTA (REAR) AND **FRENCH GREEN DRAGON** *TWO BRANDY-BASED COCKTAILS. SEE ABOVE AND PAGE 173. THE FRENCH GREEN IS, NATURALLY ENOUGH, CHARTREUSE.*

DAIQUIRI ★

1½–2 oz. light rum,
juice of ½ lime,
dash of sugar syrup or 1 teaspoon powdered sugar,
dash of maraschino (optional)

There are two styles of preparation. The mixture can be shaken very thoroughly with plenty of crushed ice, and strained into a cocktail glass. Or it can be mixed with the ice in a blender, piled up in a champagne glass, and served with a short straw. Although the ingredients and proportions vary in different recipes, the predominant tastes should be lime and rum, and the drink should taste dry and smooth. The frozen version should have the consistency of a lightly frozen water ice.

Although this name was briefly adopted as a brand by a rum distiller, it properly belongs to a classic cocktail made famous by Constante Ribalagua of La Florida restaurant, Havana, in the first half of the 20th century. He had five recipes, and there are countless others, but Daiquiri drinkers are notoriously fussy about the end result. David Embury emphasizes the importance of using lime juice, not lemon juice, although some recipes add a teaspoon of the latter, or of orange, grapefruit, or pineapple juice. Embury also cautions against allowing the oil from the peel to enter the drink (it spoils a Daiquiri but makes a Martini). Trader Vic speaks highly of Barbados rum, although, in the absence of Cuban, Puerto Rican is most commonly used. Variations include the use of two dashes of grenadine, curaçao, apricot brandy, or pineapple liqueur.

THE DAISY

1½ oz. bourbon,
1 oz. raspberry juice,
juice of ½ lemon,
½ tablespoon sugar,
soda,
raspberries,
slice of orange

Shake with ice cubes, and strain over crushed ice in a metal tankard. Top up with soda. Stir thoroughly with a barspoon until the tankard becomes very cold. Decorate with raspberries and the orange slice.

A drink of **The Sour** type which contains either raspberry syrup or grenadine and is customarily served in a metal tankard full of crushed ice, with straws. The original Daisy may have been made with gin, and many recipes use rum, but bourbon arguably works best.

DANISH GIN FIZZ

1½ oz. gin,
½ oz. Cherry Heering,
1 teaspoon kirschwasser,
2 teaspoons lime juice,
1½ teaspoons sugar syrup
Shake vigorously for some minutes with crushed ice, and strain into a chilled Highball glass. Aggressively top up with plenty of soda, and drink before it stops fizzing.

The Scandinavian element is the Cherry Heering. This distinctively dry cherry brandy is still made by the family of Peter Heering near Copenhagen.

DANNY'S SPECIAL

2 oz. whiskey,
1 oz. Cointreau,
1 teaspoon Grand Marnier,
3 tablespoons lemon juice
Stir, and serve in an Old Fashioned glass.

A good bourbon drink but why not **Jack Daniel's**?

DIABLO

1½ oz. dry white port,
1 oz. sweet vermouth,
a few drops of lemon juice
Shake with ice, and strain into a cocktail glass.

A rare opportunity to use white port. A quite different recipe is based on tequila, cassis, lime, and ginger.

DIABOLO

2 oz. rum,
½ oz. Cointreau,
½ oz. dry vermouth,
2 drops of Angostura bitters,
orange peel
Shake with, and then serve with a little crushed ice, in a cocktail glass. Garnish with a twist of orange peel.

The addition of one vowel changes **Diablo** into a rum recipe from England.

DIANA

★ ♥

2 oz. white crème de menthe or peppermint schnapps,
2 to 3 teaspoons cognac
Pack a small wine glass with crushed ice, and pour in the crème de menthe. Float the brandy on top by pouring it gently over an inverted teaspoon.

Pretty, feminine, sweet, and delightful after dinner.

DOCTOR ★ 🍸

1 oz. Swedish punsch,
1 oz. vodka (a case for Finlandia?),
1 oz. orange juice,
1 oz. lemon juice
Shake with ice cubes, and serve on the rocks in an Old Fashioned glass.

Several recipes, all based on **Swedish punsch**, with citrus juice and perhaps another spirit.

DOLORES ♥ 🍸

¾ oz. Spanish brandy,
¾ oz. cherry brandy,
¾ oz. crème de cacao
Shake with ice, and strain into a cocktail glass. Decorate with a cherry on a cocktail stick.

An opportunity to use Spanish brandy in a mixed drink. A quite different Dolores is made with Jamaica rum, dry sherry, and Dubonnet.

DRY MARTINI ★ 🍸

1 whisper dry vermouth,
1 avalanche London Dry Gin,
a touch of orange bitters (optional),
lemon zest
Stir the vermouth, gin, and orange bitters in a mixing glass amid a mountain of ice cubes, for a maximum of 30 seconds. Strain into a chilled Martini glass. Squeeze on lemon zest. Ask any drinking guests whether decorations are to be worn.

The finest of all cocktails. Subtle, potent, and a wonderful aperitif, it even has good looks. This single cocktail inspired a whole book, *Stirred – Not Shaken*, by John Doxat. He believes that the drink was invented for John D. Rockefeller by a bartender, whose name was Martini, at the Knickerbocker Hotel, New York City, in about 1910. It was originally made with French vermouth, and only later did the dry vermouth from Martini and Rossi of Italy become a favorite ingredient. How much vermouth? Doxat talks of one bartender who allegedly is content just to let the shadow of the vermouth bottle fall across the gin. Another considers it sufficient merely to bow in the direction of France while stirring the gin and ice. The

DRY MARTINI *THE DRIER THE BETTER, BUT HOW MUCH – OR HOW LITTLE – VERMOUTH HAS EXERCISED THE MINDS AND MOUTHS OF MANY A BARTENDER.*

DRY MARTINI contd.

essence of a Martini is its dryness. Doxat pours 4 oz. of vermouth (Martini Extra Dry) into a mixing glass half-filled with large ice cubes. As soon as the vermouth reaches the bottom of the glass, he pours it off and discards it. He then pours in at least 2 oz. of High and Dry gin per serving, and stirs very briskly for about 30 seconds before straining into chilled glasses. He believes enough vermouth clings to the ice to produce a ratio of 1:11 against the gin. Doxat argues that the highest acceptable proportion of vermouth to gin is 1:7, which David Embury believes to be perfect. Mixes of 1:15 and more have been known to produce excellent cocktails, and people have attempted to pass off as Martinis drinks made at 1:2. Which gin? Most Martinians like their drink, in its shivering splendor, to look almost colorless; Embury admires the golden hue imparted by the gin which is labelled simply Booth's. Lesser bars and supermarkets may have cut-rate gins that are made to a lower alcohol content, and in some brands the botanicals are infused rather than distilled; a good Martini requires plenty of alcohol and a clean, subtle, full flavor. Beefeater, Bombay, and Tanqueray score on dryness, and Gordon's scores on full flavor.

The coldness of the cocktail is also important. This can be intensified by a longer period of stirring, or Bondian shaking, but that damages by dilution. On the grounds of both appearance and dilution, Martini on the rocks is not quite the same thing. Nor is a "Vodkatini" (see **Kangaroo**).

DRY MARTINI contd.

The last essential is to cut a sliver of rind from a lemon, and squeeze it, skin-side down, over the drink. A just-visible, fine spray of oil called the zest is thus directed onto the surface of the drink. Do not float rind, or decorate with an olive unless you want a slightly oilier finish. Olives, if used, must in no circumstances be stuffed. A dash of orange bitters adds to the subtlety of the cocktail, but its drying effect has been used to disguise an unhealthily low proportion of gin.

DUBONNET CASSIS

2 oz. red Dubonnet,
1 oz. crème de cassis,
Perrier

Stir briskly in a large wine glass or an Old Fashioned glass, with a large ice cube. Top up with Perrier.

A delightfully refreshing, very French aperitif for a sunny evening.

DURANGO

1½ oz. tequila,
1½ oz. concentrated frozen grapefruit juice (undiluted),
1 teaspoon orgeat syrup or a barspoon of almond extract,
spring water,
mint sprigs

Shake with cracked ice, strain over ice cubes into an Old Fashioned or a Collins glass. Top up with spring water. Garnish with mint sprigs.

A tequila drink in which Calistoga spring water, from California, is specified by the *Complete World Bartender Guide*. Although no two spring waters are the same, Calistoga shares some properties of the most famous European examples, notably a fairly high calcium content. The spring is hot and the water – unlike Perrier – is artificially carbonated.

2 oz. Dutch jenever gin (Claeryn, if you can find it),
½ oz. Dutch curaçao,
½ oz. lemon juice,
sugar syrup to taste
Shake thoroughly with cracked ice, and strain into a cocktail glass.

DUTCH TRADE WINDS

The island of Curaçao, famous for its green oranges, was colonized by the Dutch. Hence the name of this excellent cocktail. The Dutch like their glasses filled to the brim, and bend over the bar to sip the first taste without touching the glass. If your glass is not brimful, add some more gin. Although there are many brands of Dutch gin and liqueurs, Bols is the most readily available brand outside the Netherlands.

DUTCH TRADE WINDS *A COMBINATION OF GIN AND CURAÇAO, AN ORANGE-FLAVORED LIQUEUR WHICH COMES IN A RANGE OF HUES, FROM CLEAR TO BLUE.*

EARTHQUAKE

🍸

A fun drink with tequila, or an insane mixture which is guaranteed to induce inner tremors.

1. 1½ oz. tequila,
1 teaspoon grenadine,
2 dashes of orange bitters (or Cointreau, if you prefer it sweeter),
2 strawberries,
1 orange slice

Mix in blender at high speed for 15 seconds with 3 oz. crushed ice. Strain into a cocktail glass, and decorate with strawberries and orange slice.

2. ½ oz. gin,
½ oz. bourbon,
½ oz. Pernod

Shake with ice, and strain into a cocktail glass.

EAST INDIA

★ ♥ 🍸

Shouldn't it be West Indies? Variations may be made with maraschino and raspberry syrup.

1½ oz. brandy,
¼ oz. curaçao,
¼ oz. pineapple juice,
dash of Angostura bitters

Shake with ice, and strain into a cocktail glass.

EAST INDIAN

★ 🍸

To vary, try including peach bitters, a dash of maraschino, and a mint garnish.

1½ oz. dry sherry,
1½ oz. dry vermouth,
2 dashes of orange bitters

Shake with ice, and strain into a cocktail glass.

EGG NOG NASHVILLE

Country-style seems to take a leaf out of Mrs. Beeton's book. Serves about 25.

1 pint brandy,
1 pint Jamaica rum,
1 quart bourbon,
18 eggs,
3 quarts heavy cream,
2 cups sugar,
cloves,
nutmeg

Stir liquors with egg yolks. Mix cream and sugar, and blend into liquor mixture. Beat egg whites until stiff, and fold in gently. Garnish with cloves and nutmeg. Serve in mugs.

EL PRESIDENTE ★

1½ oz. light rum,
½ oz. curaçao (optional),
½ oz. French dry vermouth,
2 dashes of grenadine
Stir or shake with ice cubes, and strain into a cocktail glass.

A distant relation of the **Daiquiri**.

ELDORADO

1 tablespoon honey,
1½ oz. lemon juice,
2 oz. tequila,
slice of orange
Shake well with cracked ice, and strain over rocks in a Collins glass. Decorate with the orange slice.

A honey-and-vitamin drink for health-food freaks who like an alcoholic kick.

EMERALD

2–3 oz. Cork gin,
1 teaspoon green crème de menthe,
a few dashes of green Pomeranz or Angostura bitters,
1 green cherry
Optional extras: lemon juice, egg white, even nutmeg, but the end result must be indisputably emerald
Shake with cracked ice, and strain into a cocktail glass. Decorate with the cherry.

Sometimes called Emerald Isle or Star. There are all sorts of variations, including one satanic recipe which threatens the drinker with rum, gin, apricot brandy, curaçao, and lemon juice, all in one glass. Surely green crème de menthe must feature? In one version it is blended in equal parts with brandy, and sometimes, diabolically, cayenne is added. This version is also known as the Erin. See also **Everybody's Irish**.

ENGLISH BISHOP see **Bishop**

ENGLISH BOLO

4 oz. dry sherry,
1½ oz. lemon juice
1 teaspoon sugar,
1 cinnamon stick
Pound the cinnamon with the lemon juice and sugar in an Old Fashioned glass. Add the sherry, and stir.

A stateless Bolo is a rather ordinary drink made with rum and fruit juices. An English one is a sherry oddity with something of a Christmas feel.

ENGLISH SHRUB see The Shrub

---

2 oz. gin,
½ oz. kirsch,
juice of ½ lemon,
1–2 teaspoons sugar,
soda
Shake well with ice cubes, and serve with 2 or 3 ice cubes in a Collins glass. Top up with soda.

ETON BLAZER

A metaphorical name, no doubt, since Eton College does not have a blazer. Nor is the college's color, black, evident in this drink. Not a Blazer in the **Blue** sense.

1½ oz. Irish whiskey,
1 teaspoon green Chartreuse,
2 dashes of green crème de menthe,
1 green olive
Stir with ice, strain into a cocktail glass, and add the olive.

EVERYBODY'S IRISH

The green olive suspended in the drink "looks like a gibbous moon," according to Harry Craddock.

1½ oz. rye,
2 dashes maraschino,
dash of orange bitters,
dash of Angostura bitters
Dip the rim of a cocktail glass into lemon juice and powdered sugar. Shake the drink with ice cubes, and strain into the glass.

FANCY FREE

An excellent rye cocktail.

1½ oz. cognac,
1½ oz. Fernet,
1 teaspoon sugar,
orange peel
Stir with lots of ice, and strain into a cocktail glass. Squeeze a sliver of orange peel over each glass, and use as decoration.

FERNET COCKTAIL

Taken as a digestif in Italy and France, and as a hangover cure in other countries, Fernet and Fernet-Branca (two different brands) still manage to find their way into the odd mixed drink. If you are feeling delicate, try a highball made with one part grenadine to three parts Fernet, and no whiskey. As a digestif, try this recipe.

FIFTH AVENUE ♥ 🍸

1 oz. dark crème de cacao,
1 oz. apricot brandy,
1 oz. sweetened cream
Use a narrow liqueur or Pousse-café glass. Pour the ingredients in gently and slowly so that they stand in layers without mixing.

A colorful and pretty drink, according to *The Savoy Cocktail Book*, but a less interesting cocktail of Fernet, gin, and vermouth if everyone else is to be believed.

FINO MARTINI 🍸

2 oz. London Dry gin,
1 teaspoon fino sherry
Prepare and serve as for Dry Martini (see page 162).

An almost acceptable variation on the great cocktail, although one authority's half-and-half mix makes this less than a Martini.

THE FIX ♥ 🥃

2 oz. London Dry gin,
¼ oz. pineapple syrup,
¼ oz. lime juice,
¼ oz. lemon juice,
dash of Cointreau,
lemon rind,
fresh pineapple pieces
Shake with crushed ice, and serve with a straw in a Highball glass. Put a substantial piece of lemon rind in the glass, and decorate with the pineapple.

A pineapple version of **The Daisy**, served in a Highball glass. That is the most clear-cut definition, although there is bored confusion about the distinction between these two Victorian categories of mixed drink. The truth is surely lost in the alcoholic mists of time.

THE FIZZ ★ 🥃

2 oz. gin,
1 oz. (or more) lemon juice,
1 oz. (or less) sugar,
soda
Shake with crushed ice, and strain into a Highball glass, straight up. Attack with soda, while stirring simultaneously. Drink immediately, while the fizzing continues.

A drink bearing this name should fizz. In order to achieve this, it may be necessary to shake the mixture for several minutes (with crushed ice), or to use a blender. It is certainly essential to employ the soda siphon with some gusto; a bottle of soda will not do. The Fizz is really a form of seltzer for the person who cannot face a drink after last night. It should be drunk at about 11:30 in the morning, before the

The Fizz *A very acceptable seltzer for the morning after the night before.*

pre-lunch cocktail. The basic fizz is made with gin, although all the other hard liquors have muscled in. Two sprigs of mint convert it into an Alabama Fizz; in a Texan version the juice of an orange quarter and a lemon quarter is added. There is much to be said for the addition of an egg white, which makes it into Silver Fizz. There is also a Golden Fizz, using egg yolk, but only the very sick or very healthy can take it. See also **Ramos Fizz**.

FJORD

2 teaspoons Norwegian Linie aquavit,
1 oz. brandy,
2 teaspoons orange juice,
2 teaspoons lime juice,
1 teaspoon grenadine
Shake well with ice, and strain on to ice cubes in an Old Fashioned glass.

The aquavit should ideally be from Norway, since that is where the fjords are.

FLAMES OVER NEW JERSEY

1 quart apple brandy,
8 oz. sugar,
a few dashes of Angostura bitters
Warm the brandy, and mix it with the sugar and bitters in a punch bowl, until completely blended. Ignite the mixture at the table, and extinguish with a large kettle of boiling water. Stir, and serve hot in mugs.

As if that unloved state has not suffered enough already. Serves about 25.

FLAMING GLÖGG

1½ pints aquavit,
1 bottle red wine,
1 cup orange juice,
cardamom seeds,
ginger root,
whole cloves,
1 cinnamon stick,
dried fruits,
grated citrus rind,
sugar to taste,
½ grapefruit

Reserve 1 cup aquavit, and mix all the other ingredients in a saucepan. Simmer thoroughly without boiling. Serve in a chafing dish.

The floating torch is the fun part. To make the floating torch, scoop the flesh out of the grapefruit half, moisten the rim and inside of the grapefruit shell with aquavit and press it in sugar. Float the shell on the glögg, fill it with the reserved aquavit until it is overflowing, and light the spirit. Let it burn for a few minutes, then overturn the shell into the glögg. Serves about ten.

FLORIDA

1¼ oz. orange juice,
½ oz. gin,
1 teaspoon kirschwasser,
1 teaspoon triple sec,
1 teaspoon lemon juice

Shake well with ice cubes, and serve on the rocks in a Collins glass.

Made with orange juice, of course. There are several variations on this recipe, including a quite different version with pineapple juice and lime juice, rum, and crème de menthe.

FLYING DUTCHMAN 

3 oz. ice-cold jenever gin,
1 teaspoon Dutch curaçao,
a dash of orange bitters

Put the curaçao into a chilled glass and swirl round. Empty the glass. Pour in the gin.

The Netherlands' answer to the Dry Martini.

FLYING SCOTSMAN

1½ oz. Scotch,
1½ oz. sweet vermouth,
dash of sugar syrup,
dash of Angostura bitters

Stir well with ice, and strain into a cocktail glass.

Would any Scot drink this ?

FRAISES FIZZ ♥

1½ oz. gin,
1 oz. strawberry liqueur,
2 teaspoons lemon juice,
1½ teaspoons sugar syrup,
twist of lemon peel,
1 strawberry
Shake well with crushed ice, and strain into a Highball glass, straight up. Add soda. Stir vigorously. Decorate with the lemon peel and strawberry.

An unusual variation on the Gin Fizz. The bartender who devised this favored the fraises (strawberry liqueur) from Chambéry.

FREDDIE FUDPUCKER ★

The tequila counterpart to a **Harvey Wallbanger**.

FRENCH GREEN DRAGON

1½ oz. cognac,
1½ oz. green Chartreuse
Shake well with crushed ice, and strain into a cocktail glass.

A ritzy after-dinner drink.

FRENCH SHERBET

¼ oz. cognac,
¼ oz. kirsch,
1 teaspoon sugar,
Angostura bitters to taste,
champagne,
cherry water ice or flavor of your choice
Stir all but the last two ingredients in a Collins glass. Top up the glass part way with champagne, then float a small scoop of water ice. Drench the water ice in champagne.

An indulgent luxury for lovers. Somehow suited to well-appointed hotel rooms.

FRISCO SOUR

2–3 oz. rye,
1 oz. Benedictine,
¼ oz. lemon juice,
¼ oz. fresh lime juice
Shake with cracked ice, and strain into a Sour glass.

An excellent whiskey cocktail, using Benedictine instead of sugar.

FROZEN BERKELEY

♥ 🍸

½ oz. California brandy,
2 teaspoons passion-fruit juice,
1½ oz. light rum

Mix in a blender with 3 oz. crushed ice at low speed for no more than 15 seconds. Strain straight up into a cocktail or champagne glass.

Many other frozen drinks, using a variety of fruits (apples, bananas, berry fruits) and different spirit bases (aquavit, tequila, brandies) can be made by the same method.

FROZEN MARGARITA

🍸

3 oz. tequila (gold makes for a fuller flavor),
1 oz. Cointreau,
1 wedge of lime,
2–3 oz. fresh lime juice,
1 scoop crushed ice,
saucer dusted with coarse salt

Take a wide-rimmed cocktail glass and moisten the edge with the lime. Upturn the glass into the salt to coat the rim. Put the tequila, Cointreau, lime juice, and ice into a blender (simple syrup may be added to taste). Serve the blended drink garnished with the wedge of lime.

The coolest version of the classic.

FROZEN MARGARITA THE SOPHISTICATE'S WAY OF DRINKING THE SPIRIT OF MEXICO THROUGH SALT AND LIME.

FUZZY NAVEL see Sex on the Beach

GAELIC COFFEE see Irish Coffee

GENOA

2 teaspoons sambuca,
2 teaspoons Martini dry vermouth,
1½ oz. grappa – Bosso Vecchio, if possible (if grappa is unavailable, use marc, or Italian brandy)

Shake with ice, and serve with 2 to 3 ice cubes in an Old Fashioned glass. Or shake without ice, and serve in a brandy snifter.

A chance to get out the sambuca. In one recipe equal parts of grappa and gin are used. Although juniper is grown in Italy, it doesn't really suit this drink.

GERMAN BAND

2 oz. (or more) Steinhäger schnapps,
¼ oz. (or less) kirschwasser or blackberry liqueur (Echte Kroatzbeere preferably),
dash of Underberg or Kabänes bitters

Refrigerate the bottle of Steinhäger. Stir the ingredients with plenty of ice in a mixing glass, and serve as for a Dry Martini, but with no decoration.

Probably a confection from Chicago, although the name is Cockney rhyming slang for "hand."

GIBSON ★

Ingredients and method as for Dry Martini (see page 162).

A Dry Martini decorated with two cocktail onions – not just one, as is often thought. This drink is supposed to be a toast to the attractive Gibson Girls.

GIMLET ★

1½ oz. London Dry or Plymouth gin,
½ oz. Rose's lime juice
Shake with ice, and strain into a cocktail glass.

There is widespread disagreement over the proportions, but the Gimlet is generally agreed to be a short gin and lime drink, while a **Rickey** is a medium or long one.

GIN FIZZ see The Fizz ★

GIN RICKEY see The Rickey ★

GIN SLING see The Sling ★

GIN AND FRENCH ★

Smart but simple cocktail which predates the Dry Martini. There is none of the ritual, just gin and French dry vermouth poured straight into a cocktail glass, with ice very optional. Proportions 1:1, or whatever suits you. The same drink with sweet vermouth is Gin and It(alian).

GINGER HIGHBALL

2 oz. bourbon,
1 large piece fresh ginger root,
soda
Pour the whiskey into a Highball glass. Squeeze the ginger on to the liquor with a garlic press. Add two to three ice cubes, and stir gently. Add soda.

Instead of using dry ginger, impress your guests with a little culinary care.

GINGER RUM TEA

1½ oz. rum,
1 cup hot tea,
1 piece of preserved ginger
Pour the rum into the tea, add the ginger and stir.

This drink can be taken hot, or it can be chilled.

GLÖGG ★

A hot wine drink in which dried fruits such as raisins and figs are used (see **Flaming Glögg**). Some other typical ingredients are blanched almonds and cardamom seeds.

GLOOM CHASER

¾ oz. curaçao,
¾ oz. Grand Marnier,
¾ oz. grenadine,
¾ oz. lemon juice
Shake well with cracked ice, and strain into a cocktail glass.

There is great confusion about both the name (see also **Gloom Lifter** and **Gloom Raiser**) and the ingredients. The basic recipe was probably Harry Craddock's. Other people add gin, dry vermouth, or sweet vermouth.

GLOOM LIFTER

2 oz. Irish whiskey,
½ oz. (or slightly more) lemon juice,
¼ oz. sugar syrup,
½ an egg white
Shake with ice, and strain into a cocktail glass.

This is probably a more efficacious mixture. In one recipe a teaspoon of brandy is added for no good reason.

GLOOM RAISER

2 oz. (or a little more) London Dry gin,
¼ oz. (or much less) French dry vermouth,
2 dashes of Pernod,
2 dashes of grenadine (optional)
Prepare and serve as for a Dry Martini (see page 162).

In this instance, does raise mean dispel or produce? No doubt the former was the intention of its creator, "Robert," of Riviera and Royal Automobile Club fame. Yet, whatever it did to London clubmen during World War I, it is a depressing way to treat a Dry Martini.

GLÜHWEIN

"Glowing Wine" in German. See **Mulled Wine**

---

1 oz. Galliano,
½ oz. white crème de cacao,
1 oz. heavy cream
Shake well with ice cubes, and strain into a cocktail glass.

GOLDEN CADILLAC ♥ 🍸

Instead of the crème de cacao, use Cointreau, with ½ oz. orange juice, and you have a Golden Dream.

---

2 oz. London Dry gin,
1 teaspoon dry vermouth,
1–2 dashes of Angostura bitters
Prepare and serve as Dry Martini (see page 162).

GOLF COCKTAIL 🍸

A Dry Martini with too much vermouth, and Angostura bitters. Use the excellent Lillet vermouth instead, and it becomes a Great Secret.

1½ oz. gin,
1 oz. passion-fruit juice (or ¼ oz. passion-fruit liqueur),
1–2 dashes of Angostura or peach bitters
Shake well with crushed ice, and strain into a cocktail glass.

GRAND PASSION 🍸

In the traditional recipe gin is used, but white rum or tequila works better.

---

1 oz. Grand Marnier,
1 teaspoon quetsch,
1 teaspoon orange juice,
1 slice of orange
Stir without ice. Pour over crushed ice into a cocktail or champagne glass. Decorate with the orange slice.

GRAND QUETSCH ♥ 🍸

A chance to use the superb white, dry brandy of the Switzen plum.

---

1 oz. grappa,
1 oz. Strega,
1 teaspoon lemon juice,
1 teaspoon orange juice
Shake with ice, and serve in a cocktail glass.

GRAPPA STREGA 🍸

An all-Italian after-dinner drink for lovers.

GREEK BUCK

1½ oz. Metaxa brandy,
1 teaspoon ouzo,
2 teaspoons lemon juice,
ginger ale

Shake the brandy and lemon juice with ice cubes and strain on to ice cubes in a Collins glass. Pour on ginger ale and float the ouzo on top.

To accompany a midafternoon honey cake, some Greek (if not Turkish) Delight, a gritty coffee, and a game of backgammon.

GREEN DRAGON

2 oz. Pernod,
2 oz. milk,
2 oz. (or less) heavy cream,
1 oz. (or less) sugar syrup

Shake with ice cubes, and strain into a chilled ballon wine glass over plenty of rocks.

One fire-breathing recipe includes gin, kümmel, crème de menthe, lemon juice, and peach bitters. Even dragons can be more civilized than that.

GREEN LADY

½ oz. green Chartreuse,
½ oz yellow Chartreuse,
¼ oz. lime juice,
1½ oz. London Dry gin (preferably Boodles),
1 slice of lime

Shake with crushed ice, and strain into a cocktail glass. Decorate with lime.

A recipe from France.

GREEN MIST

¾ oz. Galliano,
¾ oz. green Chartreuse,
¾ oz. Italian dry vermouth,
¾ oz. Italian sweet vermouth

Stir with ice cubes and strain into a cocktail glass.

A recipe from Denmark. It is better without the sweet vermouth, and with fractionally more Galliano.

GROG ★

2 oz. Jamaica rum,
1 tablespoon lemon juice,
1 sugar cube,
6 cloves, 1 cinnamon stick,
slice of lemon

Mix in a heat-proof mug with boiling water. Stir to dissolve the sugar, and add the lemon slice.

A most useful antidote for when a hot summer afternoon suddenly turns into a chilly evening. There are endless variations on the recipe.

HARVEY WALLBANGER ★

2 oz. vodka,
1 teaspoon to 2 tablespoons Galliano,
orange juice,
½ teaspoon sugar (very optional)

Shake the vodka, orange juice, and sugar, if used, with ice cubes. Pour over ice cubes into a Collins or an Old Fashioned glass, or strain into a cocktail glass. Float the Galliano on top.

The story goes that Harvey was a Californian surfer. After losing an important contest, he consoled himself excessively with his favorite drink, a **Screwdriver** with a dash of Galliano. As he left the bar, he staggered and bounced from one wall to the other. Harvey Wallbanger, they called him.

HEMINGWAY

1½ oz. absinthe (Pernod),
chilled champagne

Pour the Pernod into a champagne glass. Add champagne until it attains the proper opalescent milkiness.

Drink three or five of these slowly, said Hemingway, when he offered this recipe to *Esquire.* He mockingly called it Death in the Afternoon.

THE HIGHBALL ★

It is said that some American railroads used a signal with a ball raised on a pole to indicate to the train driver that he was running late. A highball meant "hurry." It also came to mean a simple drink that could be fixed in a hurry. The Highball has no precise definition, but it is generally agreed to mean a 1½-oz. jigger of American whiskey over 1 or 2 large ice cubes in a straight 6–8 oz. glass, topped up with soda, and given a light stir.

HONOLULU COCKTAIL

Two recipes from Trader Vic. The second one is the sweeter version.

1. 1½ oz. gin,
dash of bitters,
¼ teaspoon orange juice,
¼ teaspoon pineapple juice,
¼ teaspoon lemon juice,
½ teaspoon powdered sugar

Shake well with ice cubes, and strain into a chilled cocktail glass.

2. ¾ oz. gin,
¾ oz. maraschino,
¾ oz. Benedictine

Stir well with ice cubes, and strain into a chilled cocktail glass.

HORSE'S NECK ★

A plain Horse's Neck contains no alcohol, but a kick is normally added by using whiskey, or sometimes gin.

2½ oz. bourbon or rye,
ginger ale,
peel of a lemon, cut in a continuous spiral

Place the lemon peel inside a Collins glass, so that it curls over the edge. Put 4 large cubes of ice in the glass. Pour in the whiskey, and top up with ginger ale.

HOT BUTTERED RUM ★

The easy method is to make a hot drink with rum and spiced cider, and to stir a pat of butter into each mug. The great exponent of this drink, Trader Vic, makes a "batter" first. In Trader Vic's *Bartender Guide*, he refers to it as "our famous formula."

1½ oz. light Puerto Rican rum,
2 cups brown sugar,
½ cup softened butter,
¼–½ teaspoon ground nutmeg,
¼–½ teaspoon ground cinnamon,
¼–½ teaspoon ground cloves,
pinch of salt,
1 8-inch cinnamon stick

Beat the sugar and butter together until they are thoroughly creamed and fluffy. Beat in the nutmeg, cinnamon, cloves and salt. Put a heaped teaspoon of this "batter" in each mug. Add the rum, top up with hot water, stir well, and mull with a hot poker. Decorate with the cinnamon stick.

HOT RUM COW

1 teaspoon powdered sugar,
dash of Angostura bitters,
dash of vanilla essence,
8 oz. very hot milk,
1½ oz. light Puerto Rican rum,
grated nutmeg

Mix thoroughly in a blender. Pour into a large heated mug. Dust with nutmeg.

Milky alcoholic drinks seem to have become known as Cows. This one is another of Trader Vic's variations.

ICEBERG

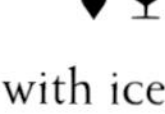

1 oz. Galliano,
2 teaspoons Cointreau,
2 oz. orange water ice

Mix in blender until smooth, and serve in a stemmed narrow glass (Parfait or Pousse-café), with a straw.

Nearly all liqueurs are delicious with ice cream or water ice. Strega flavors a famous Italian ice cream, and here its rival Galliano suffuses a water ice.

ICEBREAKER

2 oz. tequila,
2 oz. grapefruit juice,
1 tablespoon grenadine,
2 teaspoons Cointreau,
4 oz. crushed ice

Mix in blender at low speed for 15 seconds, and strain into a Sour glass straight up.

In one recipe this name is bestowed upon a rum-laced tea; in another it is given to a Daiquiri-ish tequila drink.

ICED COFFEE FILLIP

8 oz. very strong black coffee,
2 teaspoons Tia Maria or Kahlúa

Stir thoroughly, and chill until ice-cold.

Many liqueurs make delicious additions to iced coffee. Try also crème de cacao, kirsch, or crème de menthe. For a kick with a flavor, try using Jamaica rum or Irish whiskey.

INDEPENDENCE DAY PUNCH

What to drink on July 4? One answer is 2 quarts bourbon, mixed with 1 pint pineapple juice, 8 oz. lime juice, and soda. The response here is more elaborate. Serves 15.

1 bottle chilled champagne,
1 bottle cognac,
3 bottles dry red wine,
1 pint strong tea,
juice of 2 dozen lemons,
6 cups powdered sugar,
lemon slices

Dissolve the sugar in the lemon juice in a large punch bowl. Add the tea, and large chunks of ice, then the wine and cognac. Chill thoroughly. Immediately before serving, pour in the champagne. Serve in wine goblets. Decorate with the lemon slices.

IRISH COFFEE ★

Although Irish whiskey is a wonderful spirit in its own right, its worldwide reputation is owed to the invention of Gaelic Coffee. Today, every other spirit is used in hot coffee drinks, but none works better than Irish. This case is put concisely by Brian Murphy, an Englishman despite his name, in his *World Book of Whisky*: "Some magic in the flavors of coffee and Irish whiskey produces a taste quite different from either, but within which you can still distinguish the original elements." In the days when transatlantic airplanes had to stop for fuel at Shannon, the weather in the wild west of Ireland was fought with Gaelic Coffee in the airport bar, whence the habit spread to the United States. The great authority Harry Grossman supports the claim of the Buena Vista Café, Fisherman's Wharf, San Francisco, to have pioneered Irish Coffee in the Americas, but doubtless there are many other contenders.

1 teaspoon sugar,
1½ oz. Irish whiskey,
5 oz. very strong, scalding-hot black coffee made from freshly ground beans,
heavy cream

Rinse an 8 oz. stemmed goblet with hot water. Place the sugar in the glass, followed by the whiskey. Add the coffee, leaving enough room for the cream. Stir thoroughly, and wait until the surface is calm before adding the cream by pouring it very slowly over the back of a teaspoon. The cream must float on top of the coffee, and not blend into the drink. If you fail, don't serve the drink to your guests; knock it back quickly yourself, and try again.

IRISH COW ♥

The heavy cream, chocolate-flavored whiskey made by Bailey's of Dublin, makes a superb nightcap in a hot milk drink.

ISLAND BREEZE

1½ oz. white rum,
2 dashes Angostura bitters,
4 oz. pineapple juice,
1 oz. cranberry juice
Build over ice in a Highball glass.

One of several 1990s creations by Dale Degroff, the star shaker and mixer at the Rainbow Room, atop New York's Rockefeller Plaza.

JACK ROSE ★

2 oz. apple brandy,
juice of 1 lime (or less),
dash of grenadine (or more)
Shake with ice, and strain into a cocktail glass.

The best-known applejack drink, very similar to the **Applejack Rabbit**.

JACKIE O'S ROSE

2 oz. light rum,
1 oz. lime juice,
dash of Cointreau,
sugar to taste
Serve as Jack, or over crushed ice in a Sour glass.

Same principle as Jack, but different ingredients. It may need sweetening with a little sugar.

JAMAICA GINGER BEER

5 oz. Jamaican ginger,
2 oz. honey,
2 oz. lime juice,
1 egg white,
3 cups sugar,
½ oz. fresh or ¼ oz. dry yeast,
several drops of Angostura bitters
Pound the ginger. Mix the ginger, sugar, honey, and lime juice with 2 quarts water in a large jug. Dissolve the yeast in a spoonful of water and add with the beaten egg white. Stir to blend.

This is worth the trouble. Ginger beer is altogether different from ginger ale. It needs to stand in a cool, dark place. After a few days, bubbling should indicate the beginnings of fermentation. After several more days, this should cease, indicating that the ginger beer is ready. Strain through cheesecloth before serving or bottling. Sweeten the beer to taste.

JAMAICAN SHANDY

2 cans lager,
1 pint ginger beer
Stir gently over 2 ice cubes in large stemmed glasses.

For Jamaican Shandy it is essential to use Jamaican Ginger Beer with Red Stripe, a very light and quenching Jamaican lager beer. Serves two.

JAPANESE COCKTAIL ★

2 oz. cognac,
1 teaspoon almond extract or ¼ oz. orgeat,
1 or more dashes of Angostura bitters,
1 teaspoon lime juice (optional),
sliver of lemon peel
Shake with cracked ice, and strain into a cocktail glass. Decorate with the lemon peel.

This is a recognized recipe, although a more Japanese drink would be an Alexander made with Suntory whiskey and green tea liqueur.

JOCKEY CLUB ★

2 oz. gin,
2 dashes of crème de noyau,
4 dashes of lemon juice,
orange bitters and Angostura bitters to taste
Shake thoroughly with ice cubes, and strain into a cocktail glass.

One authority maintains that this is a sweet Manhattan with two dashes of maraschino to each drink. The Savoy version is more commonly accepted.

JOHN COLLINS see The Collins ★

JULEP see Mint Julep ★

KAHLÚA JAVA

2 pints hot coffee,
2 pints hot cocoa,
1 oz. (or more) Kahlúa,
marshmallows
Stir in a chafing dish, and serve in mugs, each one topped with a marshmallow.

A thoroughly sickly treat. Serves eight.

KANGAROO ★ 🍸

1½ oz. vodka,
¾ oz. dry vermouth,
twist of lemon peel (optional)
Stir with ice, and serve straight up in a cocktail glass, or on the rocks in an Old Fashioned glass, with a twist of lemon peel.

The facts are that Australians drink beer, and the spirit historically connected with their homeland is rum, but this vodka cocktail is universally accepted as a Kangaroo. It is a less offensive name than Vodkatini.

KENTUCKY COLONEL ★ 🍸

1½ oz. bourbon,
2 teaspoons Benedictine
Stir with ice, and serve on the rocks in an Old Fashioned glass.

This name is sometimes given to a mix of bourbon and pineapple juice, although that is surely the unranked version.

KERRY COOLER

2 oz. Irish whiskey,
1 oz. dry sherry,
1 tablespoon almond extract,
1 tablespoon (or more) lemon juice,
soda,
slice of lemon
Shake well with ice cubes. Serve on the rocks in a Collins glass, topped up with soda, and decorated with the lemon slice.

Nothing as disgusting as this could have come from the kingdom of Kerry.

KINGSTON 🍸

1 oz. Jamaica rum,
2 teaspoons kümmel,
2 teaspoons orange juice,
1 dash of pimento liqueur
Shake well with ice cubes, and strain into a cocktail glass.

One widely accepted recipe is for a nasty mixture of rum, gin, lime or lemon juice, and optional grenadine. This one is bizarre, but no less workable.

Kentucky Colonel *(front)* and **The Highball** (see page 180). *Two cocktails which can be fixed in a hurry.*

1 teaspoon to 2 tablespoons crème de cassis (or blackcurrant juice),
4 oz. chilled white burgundy
Pour the wine over the blackcurrant juice in a ballon wine glass. Ice optional.

KIR

A very popular and agreeable French aperitif, named after Canon Kir, heroic wartime mayor of Dijon, and left-wing politician.

---

2 oz. crème de cassis,
1 oz. kirsch,
soda
The French just pour and stir, but there is much to be said for shaking with cracked ice, to cool thoroughly and slightly dilute. Serve in a ballon wine glass with 2 or 3 ice cubes. Top up with soda.

KIRSCH AND CASSIS

A very sweet but typically French drink for warm afternoons at the pavement café.

---

1 teaspoon raspberry syrup,
1 teaspoon lemon or lime juice,
1 teaspoon orange juice,
½ teaspoon curaçao (optional),
2 oz. light rum
Optional: 1 teaspoon of pineapple juice or crushed pineapple and/or a slice of pineapple as decoration
Shake very thoroughly with crushed ice and strain into a cocktail glass.

KNICKERBOCKER

The regular version of this cocktail is a rather ordinary mixture of gin with two teaspoons of dry vermouth and one of sweet vermouth. The Special is a drinker's fruit salad.

1½–2 oz. bourbon,
½ teaspoon (or more) Pernod,
½ teaspoon (or less) anisette,
2 dashes (or more) of Angostura bitters,
pineapple pieces
Stir with ice cubes, and strain into a cocktail glass. Decorate with pineapple.

LADIES' COCKTAIL

A quaint name which is evidence of bartenders' prejudices, but there is nothing especially gentle about the drink.

LAGUNA

2 oz. Italian brandy,
¼ oz. vodka,
¼ oz. Martini bianco,
1 teaspoon Campari,
dash of amaro (Italian bitters),
1 maraschino cherry

Shake with ice cubes, and serve in a cocktail glass, decorated with the cherry.

Suitable for Beach Boys, even though it comes from Italy.

LEAVE IT TO ME

1 oz. London Dry or Plymouth gin,
½ oz. dry vermouth,
½ oz. apricot brandy,
dash of grenadine,
dash of lemon juice

Shake with ice, and strain into a cocktail glass.

To whom? There is another version which includes raspberry liqueur and maraschino.

LIBERAL

1½ oz. Canadian whisky,
1½ oz. sweet vermouth,
3 dashes of Amer Picon,
dash of orange bitters

Shake with ice cubes and serve with ice in an Old Fashioned glass.

This can be made drier with less sweet vermouth and more Picon.

LIBERTY ★

1½ oz. apple brandy,
1 tablespoon (or more) white rum,
a few drops of sugar syrup

Stir with ice, and strain into a cocktail glass.

Another version blends 1½ oz. of apricot brandy with ½ to 1 oz. sloe gin.

LILLET COCKTAIL

1½ oz. Lillet,
1 tablespoon dry gin,
twist of lemon

Stir with ice. Serve with the twist of lemon in a cocktail glass or in an Old Fashioned glass.

This makes use of a delicate vermouth which deserves a bigger reputation. Add a teaspoon of crème de noyau for a yet more interesting aperitif.

LIMEY

1 oz. light rum,
1½ tablespoons lime liqueur,
***2 teaspoons* triple sec,**
2 teaspoons lime juice,
1 slice of lime

Mix in a blender at low speed for 15 seconds with 3 oz. crushed ice. Strain into a saucer-shaped champagne glass. Decorate with the sliver of lime.

Liqueurs made from limes are not always easy to find. Spain has one called Crema de Lima.

LONG ISLAND ICED TEA

½ oz. tequila,
½ oz. white rum,
½ oz. vodka,
½ oz. gin,
***½ oz.* triple sec,**
1 oz. lemon juice and 1 teaspoon sugar (or substitute sweet 'n' sour mix),
cola

Stir over ice, strain into a Collins glass filled with ice cubes, top up

A disarming name for a tall and potent drink combining more than one innocently white spirit (usually in equal parts), sometimes flavoring them with a *triple sec* such as Cointreau, and hiding them in cola. This is Long Island Iced Tea at its most extreme.

LOS ANGELES

1½ oz. bourbon,
dash of Italian sweet vermouth,
1–1½ teaspoons sugar,
1 egg

Shake with ice cubes, and strain into a small saucer-shaped champagne glass, or serve on the rocks in an Old Fashioned glass.

The ingredients are familiar. Just add an egg.

LOUISIANA LULLABY

1½ oz. dark rum,
2 teaspoons dark Dubonnet,
2–3 drops Grand Marnier,
sliver of lemon

Stir with ice, and strain into a cocktail glass. Decorate with the sliver of lemon.

This is appropriately Francophile.

MADEIRA MINT FLIP ♥ 🍸

A rare chance to use madeira – and chocolate mint liqueur.

1½ oz. madeira,
1 tablespoon chocolate mint liqueur,
1½ teaspoons (or less) sugar syrup,
1 egg,
grated nutmeg,
grated dark chocolate

Shake very thoroughly with ice, and strain into a cocktail glass. Decorate with the nutmeg or grated chocolate.

MAI-TAI ★ 🥃

The name is similar to that of a malodorous Chinese liquor, but sweet Mai-Tai is now a classic cocktail.

1 lime,
½ oz. curaçao,
¼ oz. rock candy syrup (or sugar),
¼ oz. orgeat syrup,
2 oz. Trader Vic Mai-Tai rum or 1 oz. dark Jamaica rum and 1 oz. light or medium rum (preferably Martinique),
peel of 1 lime,
pineapple pieces,
cocktail cherries or fresh mint sprigs

Squeeze the lime juice over shaved ice in an Old Fashioned or Collins glass. Add the other ingredients. Decorate with the lime peel, the pineapple and the cherry, or mint.

MAI-TAI A TROPICAL FRUIT AND RUM SALAD IN A GLASS, AND NOW A CLASSIC COCKTAIL.

MANHATTAN ★

2½ oz. rye,
1 oz. Italian sweet vermouth
Angostura bitters
Stir well with ice cubes, and strain into a cocktail glass. Decorate with a maraschino cherry.

One of the basic cocktails, usually made with rye, although some drinkers prefer bourbon. Bitters are essential. Some drinkers also like to have a drop of orange bitters. Others prefer a sweetener like maraschino cherry juice. Like all classics, the Manhattan inspires great debate as to exactly which ingredients, and in what proportion, make the true cocktail. The recipe here is for a regular Manhattan. A Dry Manhattan employs only French vermouth and is decorated with a twist of lemon; a Perfect has the same amount of vermouth, but half Italian sweet and half French dry; a Sweet has Italian vermouth only.

MARGARITA ★

1–2 oz. tequila,
½ oz. triple sec
(preferably Cointreau),
juice of ½ a lime
Shake very thoroughly with cracked ice, or use a blender. Strain into a cocktail or saucer-shaped champagne glass rimmed with salt.

A modern classic.

MARTINI see **Dry Martini**

MAYAN WHORE

1½ oz. tequila,
1 oz. Kahlúa,
3 oz. chilled pineapple juice,
soda
Pour first the tequila, then the pineapple juice. Top up with soda and float the Kahlúa on top. Do not stir. Let it stand like a layered Pousse-café, and drink through a straw.

From down Mexico way, or just from southern California? In fact, the recipe comes from the Jerome Hotel, Aspen, Colorado.

MERRY WIDOW ★ 🍸

1½ oz. Dubonnet,
1½ oz. French vermouth
Stir well with ice, and strain into a cocktail glass. Add a twist of lemon peel, and the drink is metamorphosed from a Mary Garden into a Merry Widow. Or, instead of the lemon peel, add a dash of orange bitters. An excellent aperitif.

A quite different, and much sweeter, Merry Widow (♥) is made with 1½ oz. cherry brandy and 1½ oz. maraschino, shaken.
Serve with ice in a cocktail glass topped with a cherry.

Is it the need to drown sorrows, or the imagined availability of the widow, that make this name so popular among cocktail bartenders? There are several variations, all of them standard cocktails.

An ungarnished Merry Widow is called a Mary Garden.

Merry Widow Fizz (▮) is the same as **Gin Fizz**, but half of the lemon juice is replaced by orange juice.

Merry Widower (🍸) is made with:
1½ oz. London Dry gin, 1½ oz. dry French vermouth, 2 dashes of Pernod, a dash of bitters, and 2 dashes of Benedictine.
Shake, strain over ice, and serve with a twist of lemon peel, in a cocktail glass.

MIDORI SOUR

2–3 oz. Midori,
½–2 oz. white rum,
1 oz. cream
Shake, and strain into a chilled Sour glass.

The Japanese melon liqueur Midori is one of the world's more unusual drinks, but how to use it? This concoction is not a sour in the classic sense, but that is what it's called.

MILK PUNCHES ▮

2–3 oz. whisky or brandy of choice,
½ pint milk,
1 teaspoon sugar
Shake with cracked ice until blended, then strain into a long glass. Dust with nutmeg, and decorate with orange peel. Or, for a most effective nightcap, mix the liquor and sugar, then pour into a mug or a glass with a handle followed by hot (but not boiling) milk.

White Flush is a milk punch made with gin, and sometimes with maraschino instead of sugar.

Bull's Milk is made with 2 parts rum to 3 parts brandy.

Tiger's Milk is an ambitious drink made with applejack, sugar, ½ an egg white, a hint of vanilla essence, the same of orange essence, a clove and a piece of cinnamon. The egg white is beaten, then shaken with the flavorings, liquor, and ice, strained into a long glass, and topped with equal proportions of milk and sweet cider. Clench your stomach, and swallow for dear life.

MIMOSA see **Buck's Fizz**

MINT JULEP ★

Redolent of the South, with pulchritudinous young women lolling provocatively on the porch, or in a swing, waiting for a long drink to cool, or inflame, passions. Different passions are inflamed over the merits of various mixing techniques. As always, it is a matter of taste. Frost a long glass in the refrigerator before you start.

4 mint sprigs,
1 teaspoon or cube of sugar,
a swoosh of soda or ½ a small cup of water, crushed ice,
2–3 oz. bourbon

Take at least a dozen small, tender leaves from two of the mint sprigs and muddle them gently with the sugar, in a bar glass. Pour on the bourbon and soda or water, and stir gently until the sugar is completely dissolved. Strain into the frosted glass packed with crushed ice. Stir with a long spoon. Rinse the remaining mint sprigs in cold water, dry them with a clean towel, dip them in powdered sugar, clip the ends of the stems to release juice, and immerse them in the glass as a garnish. Serve with straws. Some bartenders add 3 dashes of Angostura to the mixing glass. Some top the drink with a splash of rum. Some argue passionately against any stirring.

MOJITO ★

A rum **Collins**, with sprigs of mint.

MINT JULEP *(FRONT) AND* **OLD FASHIONED** *(SEE PAGE 197). TWO CLASSIC WHISKEY COCKTAILS. THE WHISKEY MUST BE AMERICAN.*

MONKEY GLAND ★

1½ oz. gin,
1 generous tablespoon fresh orange juice,
a generous few drops of Benedictine, and the same again of grenadine

Stir with ice in a mixing glass, then strain into an Old Fashioned glass, over plenty of ice.

Not a steak, but a refreshing short cocktail. A good aperitif if the mix is not too sweet.

MONTANA ★

2 oz. brandy,
2 teaspoons port,
2 teaspoons dry vermouth

Stir, and serve with one cube of ice in a cocktail glass.

Perhaps a restorative in the mountain cold, and a marvellous antidote for sickly stomachs or weak knees.

MOSCOW MULE ★

2–3 oz. vodka,
juice of ½ a lime,
twist of lime peel,
ginger ale (or preferably ginger beer),
cucumber peel

Add two ice cubes, stir and serve in a Collins glass. Garnish with the cucumber peel.

An American invention, of course. A very refreshing long cocktail, and you can vary the amount of vodka to adjust the kick of the mule.

MOUNT FUJI

1½ oz. light rum,
1½ oz. applejack,
1 oz. Southern Comfort,
1 oz. sugar,
juice of ½ a lime,
crushed ice
For the flambéed finale:
1 oz. of 75% (151 proof) rum,
the scooped-out shell of the ½ lime

Combine the ingredients in a blender to produce an icy, alcoholic lava, and empty this into a Sour glass, or something more elaborate, to make a mountain.

An explosive standard cocktail, but this spectacular version is from the Beverly Hilton. For the finale, place the scooped-out lime shell on top of the "mountain," inverted like a crater, fill with the explosive rum, ignite and admire the volcanic scene. As the heat melts the icy lava, drink with a straw.

MULLED WINE

2 bottles red wine,
¼ bottle port,
¼ bottle brandy,
peel of 1 orange and 1 lemon,
grated nutmeg,
6 cloves,
1 or 2 pieces of cinnamon,
1 tablespoon brown sugar

Bring all the ingredients almost to a boil, stirring with a wooden spoon, and simmer for 5 minutes. Serve in mugs.

Fun for a party, and almost obligatory after skiing. Serves about six.

NEGRONI

★

2 oz. dry gin,
1 oz. sweet Italian vermouth,
1 oz. Campari,
slice of orange

Pour over large cubes of ice in a ballon wine glass. Stir well. Add the orange slice.

An elegant aperitif, with a vaguely Broadway flavor.

OLD FASHIONED

★

2 teaspoons sugar syrup,
3 dashes of bitters,
1½ oz. rye,
twist of lemon,
slice of orange

Pour sugar syrup and bitters into an Old Fashioned glass and stir thoroughly with a spoon. Add the ice, top up with whiskey, and stir again.

A classic whiskey cocktail, for which there are countless recipes. The whiskey must be American, and some argue specifically for rye. Some argue that the sugar should be in the form of syrup; others accept cubes muddled with water. Some hold out for Angostura bitters; others favor Péychaud. Some drinkers like a swoosh of soda; others object.

Add a twist of lemon to the drink. Garnish with a slice of orange and, if you must, a maraschino cherry. An Old Fashioned can be agreeably embellished with a dash of curaçao.

OLYMPIA

★ 🍸

1 teaspoon cherry brandy, usually Danish,
1 oz. fresh lime juice,
2 oz. rum
Stir well with plenty of ice, and strain into a cocktail glass.

Dark rum is preferred in the classic recipe for this cocktail but a light rum version is also popular.

OLYMPIC

★ 🍸

¾ oz. brandy,
¾ oz. curaçao,
¾ oz. (or vary to taste) fresh orange juice
Stir well with plenty of ice, and strain into a cocktail glass.

A delightfully refreshing cocktail to round off lunch on a warm summer day.

ONE IRELAND

♥ 🍸

1 oz. Irish whiskey,
1 tablespoon crème de menthe,
2 oz. vanilla ice cream
Mix thoroughly in a blender. Serve in a cocktail glass.

A Republican ambition, of course, as can be seen by the color of the ingredients. Do not ask for this drink in the wrong part of Belfast. Otherwise delicious on a rare hot afternoon in any of the 32 counties.

OPENING

♥ 🍸

1 oz. rye (some bartenders prefer Canadian),
2 teaspoons sweet vermouth,
2 teaspoons grenadine
Shake with ice, and serve over plenty of ice in an Old Fashioned glass. Some bartenders prefer to stir.

A classic cocktail, with interesting flavors, but rather sweet. Another Opening, another show?

OPERA

★ 🍸

1½ oz. gin, preferably London Dry,
1 teaspoon (or more, to taste) Dubonnet,
1 teaspoon maraschino
Optional extras: orange peel, or the tiniest squeeze of juice.
Shake well with ice, and strain into a cocktail glass. Decorate with orange peel or a slice of orange.

A sophisticated cocktail to drink before a night with the Marx Brothers.

ORANGE BLOOM

There are at least 20 mixed drinks in which orange is the dominant flavor, but the classic variations are the Blossom, the Fizz and the Bloom.

1 oz. gin, preferably London Dry,
2 teaspoons Cointreau,
2 teaspoons Italian sweet vermouth

Shake with ice, and strain over ice into a cocktail glass.

ORANGE BLOSSOM

This is sometimes known as the Adirondack. Originally, in the Prohibition period, a modest blush of orange was used to disguise an enormous slug of gin, and there was nothing more to it. Today, a more civilized version is in order and there are a great many amusing variations.

1½ oz. gin,
½ oz. orange juice,
2 teaspoons curaçao (optional),
2 teaspoons fresh lemon or fresh lime juice,
a couple of drops of orange-flower water,
1 teaspoon sugar syrup,
slice of orange

Shake with plenty of ice, or use a blender, in which case an egg white may be added. Strain and serve in a Sour glass with plenty of ice. Add the orange slice.

ORANGE FIZZ

A variation on the **Gin Fizz**.

2 oz. gin,
2 tablespoons lemon juice,
2 teaspoons triple sec,
1½ teaspoons sugar syrup,
2 dashes of orange bitters,
soda,
orange juice,
slice of orange

Shake with ice. Strain into a Sour glass. Add ice and soda, a squeeze of orange, and the orange slice.

PARADISE

★

Sometimes mixed with light rum, but more commonly with gin.

1½ oz. (or more) gin,
1 oz. orange juice,
1 oz. (or less) apricot brandy

Shake with cracked ice, and strain into a cocktail glass. Decorate with a thin slice of orange.

PARK LANE SPECIAL

2 oz. gin,
⅔ oz. apricot brandy (liqueur),
juice of ½ a fresh orange,
dash of grenadine,
½ an egg white
Shake with ice, and strain into a cocktail glass.

From the Park Lane Hotel, London. With British eccentricity, the aforesaid hotel is not quite in Park Lane, but nearby in Piccadilly.

PEACH WEST INDIES

1½ oz. light rum,
½ peach,
2–3 drops of Rose's lime juice,
2–3 drops maraschino
Peel the peach, and combine with the other ingredients and 3 oz. crushed ice in a blender at high speed for 15 seconds. Strain into a small saucer-shaped champagne glass.

Add crème de banane if you want to change the flavor.

PEPPERMINT PARK

2 oz. gin,
1 oz. sweetened lemon juice,
champagne
Shake the gin and juice thoroughly with ice cubes, and strain into a large champagne saucer. Top up with champagne, and serve with straws.

Bright young things and ardent Americanophiles flock to Peppermint Park in London to feed off pastrami on rye (bread, not whiskey), and dig into dazzling cocktails.

PICON see **Amer Picon**

PIMM'S

3 oz. Pimm's No. 1,
1 twist cucumber peel,
1 slice of lemon,
a few borage leaves,
plenty of ice,
fizzy lemonade or 7-Up
Optional:
1 oz. London Dry or Plymouth gin,
1 teaspoon Cointreau
Serve in a 1-pint glass mug.

The invention of James Pimm who ran a restaurant in London in the 1880s. Pimm devised a gin sling which was so peculiar that he put it into commercial production. His celebrated product, gin flavored with herbs and liqueurs, anticipated the packaged cocktail by over a hundred years. Pimm's No. 2 (whisky-based), No. 3 (brandy), No. 4 (rum), and No. 5 (rye) are no longer produced, but No. 6 (vodka) is still available. Although it features in a variety of confections, Pimm's is a mixed drink in itself, and merely needs serving properly.

PIÑA COLADA ★ ♥ ▮

2–3 oz. golden rum,
3–4 oz. crushed pineapple, or pineapple juice,
1½–2 oz. cream of coconut,
pineapple pieces

Shake, or mix in a blender, with 1 scoop of shaved ice. Pour over more ice in a Collins glass, and serve with a straw. Decorate with the pineapple pieces.

Among the mixed drinks which have established themselves in the 1970s, surely none has won such widespread popularity as the Piña Colada.

PINK GIN 🍸

1½ oz. Plymouth gin,
several drops of Angostura bitters

Shake the bitters into a wine or Martini glass, roll them around, and shake out. Pour in the gin. Ice optional.

The lingering flavor of smart London – Park Lane, Berkeley Square, and the watering holes of Mayfair between the wars and in the 1940s – although this "sophisticated" drink originated as a medicinal potion in the British navy.

PISCO PUNCH ★ ▮

3 oz. Pisco brandy,
1½ teaspoons sugar syrup,
1 teaspoon lime juice,
1 egg white,
Angostura bitters

Shake everything but the bitters with ice cubes, strain into a Sour glass, then add the bitters.

A rare opportunity to use the Pisco brandy of Peru.

PLANTER'S PUNCH ★

Made with Myers rum, from Jamaica. A classic mixed drink, though recipes vary.

1½ oz. (or more) Jamaica rum,
juice of ½ lemon or lime
3 oz. orange juice (optional)
1 teaspoon sugar,
soda,
slice of orange

Shake well with crushed ice, and pour into a Collins glass. Top up the glass with more ice and a squirt of soda. Churn with a barspoon. Decorate with the orange slice.

PLANTER'S PUNCH *PUNCHES ARE A GREAT FAVORITE FOR PARTIES, THE ADVANTAGE BEING THAT THEY CAN BE PREPARED IN ADVANCE.*

POUSSE-CAFÉ ★♥🍸

Strictly "our next trick is impossible," according to John Doxat. A Pousse-café is a series of liqueurs in different colors floating on top of each other in the glass. Very sickly, but spectacular if it can be done. Keep the glass very still, and pour the liqueurs over a spoon. Different liqueurs have different weights, and they must be poured in ascending order of lightness. David Embury suggests the following order: 1. grenadine; 2. brown crème de cacao; 3. maraschino; 4. orange curaçao; 5. green crème de menthe; 6. parfait amour; 7. cognac.

Use a straight-sided Pousse-café glass, of course.

Pousse-cafés enjoyed a revival in the 1980s and 1990s, as a variation on the **Shooter**. A typical new-generation Pousse-café is Altered States, in which pear liqueur is layered over Bailey's Irish Cream and Kahlúa.

PRESIDENT see **El Presidente** ★

---

1 oz. lemon juice,
2 oz. orange juice,
1 teaspoon grenadine,
½ egg yolk,
1 cherry

Shake thoroughly with cracked ice, and pour into a wine glass with one or two ice cubes. Decorate with the cherry.

PUSSYFOOT ★

A non-alcoholic cocktail, for an abstaining guest who does not wish to be conspicuous. Several of these drinks were created during the Prohibition era. One modern Pussyfoot has gone back on the bottle, with rum.

QUEBEC

1½ oz. Canadian whisky,
2 teaspoons Noilly Prat dry vermouth,
1 teaspoon Amer Picon,
1 teaspoon maraschino

Stir with ice in a mixing glass, and serve in a cocktail glass, or an Old Fashioned glass.

Say Noilly Prat, and your Canadian is perfect.

RAMOS FIZZ ★

1½ oz. gin,
¼ cup half-and-half milk and heavy cream,
1 egg white,
juice of ½ large lemon,
1 heaped teaspoon sugar,
1 teaspoon orange-flower water

Shake with crushed ice and strain into a Highball glass.

The morning-after drink before Sunday brunch. A New Orleans Gin Fizz with orange-flower water. Minor variations abound. This recipe comes from Victor, of Ginsberg's Dublin Pub, at Mason and Bay, San Francisco. (Oy Vay, Mason and Bay.)

THE RICKEY ★

2 oz. dry gin,
1 oz. fresh lime or lemon juice
1 or more dashes of grenadine,
long twist of lime peel,
soda

Mix the ingredients with one cube of ice in an Old Fashioned glass. Immerse a substantial twist of peel. Top up with soda, and stir very thoroughly with a barspoon.

A medium-sized drink usually flavored with lime, most commonly based on gin and made to a fairly dry mix. Invented by a "Colonel" Rickey, from Kentucky.

ROSE OF WARSAW ♥

1½ oz. Wyborowa Polish vodka,
1 oz. Wisniak cherry liqueur,
½ oz. Cointreau,
dash of Angostura bitters

Stir with ice in a mixing glass, and serve in a cocktail glass.

A recipe from Paris, actually.

ROAD RUNNER ♥ 🍸

1 oz. vodka,
½ oz. Amaretto,
½ oz. coconut juice,
nutmeg

Shake thoroughly with cracked ice, and strain into a cocktail glass. Sprinkle with nutmeg.

From Al Arteaga, Cathedral Canyon Country Club, Palm Springs.

RUSTY NAIL ★ 🍸

1½ oz. Scotch whisky,
1 oz. Drambuie

Serve in a cocktail glass without ice, floating the Drambuie on top, or in an Old Fashioned glass with a couple of ice cubes.

Some suggest proportions of 1:1. Even 2:1 produces too sticky a drink. Do not stir, not even with a rusty nail.

SANGAREE

1 teaspoon icing sugar,
1 large glass sherry or port,
slice of orange or a twist of lemon peel, and nutmeg

Stir well, and strain into an Old Fashioned glass. Add orange slice or lemon peel, and dust with nutmeg.

Originally a sweetened fortified wine served in a tumbler, and often iced. An old Anglicization of the Spanish word Sangria. This is the Savoy Sangaree.

SANGRIA ★

1 bottle Spanish dry red wine,
2 oz. Spanish brandy,
1 oz. curaçao or similar liqueur,
3 oz. lemon juice,
3 oz. orange juice,
2 oz. sugar,
½ orange, sliced

Stir ingredients in a jug, and serve in large wine glasses.

An essential part of a holiday in Spain. Serves four.

THE SCAFFA ★

An old term, the meaning of which is no longer clear. Generally agreed to be a drink in which a spirit and a liqueur share a glass with a dash of bitters, but there is doubt over a Pousse-café dimension. Brandy maraschino, and perhaps green Chartreuse are candidates for inclusion.

SCORPION ★

2 oz. light, golden or (for an extra sting) Barbadian rum,
1 oz. inexpensive brandy,
½ oz. orgeat syrup,
2 oz. orange juice,
1½ oz. lemon juice

Mix with two scoops of crushed ice in a blender. Serve on the rocks in a ballon or Highball glass with a decorative straw or two and a couple of thin slices of orange. Trader Vic's gardenia garnish is strictly for San Franciscans.

One of the newer generation of long refreshing drinks that is also perilously alcoholic. They all hint at Californian (and, these days, Texan) recklessness, yet several are, despite their youth, already universal "old" standards. The Scorpion certainly is. Trouble is that they are so potent and fruity that it can be hard to tell them apart.

SCREWDRIVER ★

1½ oz. vodka,
orange juice to taste

Pour the vodka into an Old Fashioned or Collins glass, with plenty of ice, and add the juice. Stir.

Supposedly invented by oilmen who stirred it with their screwdrivers.

SEX ON THE BEACH

1 oz. vodka,
1 oz. peach schnapps,
dash of blackberry liqueur (optional),
2 oz. cranberry juice,
2 oz. orange juice,
2 oz. pineapple juice (optional)

This drink is also sometimes shaken and served as a Shooter.

This is a good example of the many cocktails that were provoked by the fashion for peach "schnapps" (actually, liqueurs) in the 1980s and 1990s. Sex on the Beach involves vodka, peach schnapps, and more than one fruit juice. A version made only from vodka, peach schnapps, and orange juice is known as the Fuzzy Navel.

SHAMROCK

Variation on **Everybody's Irish**, with vermouth.

SCREWDRIVER *A BASIC ORANGE-JUICE AND VODKA COCKTAIL WHICH IS PRIMARILY ORANGE-FLAVORED.*

SHIRLEY TEMPLE

A dash of grenadine in a large champagne glass full of 7-Up or ginger ale, decorated with cherries. No alcohol.

A kids' cocktail.

SHOOTERS

¾ oz. Kahlúa,
½ oz. Bailey's Irish Cream,
1 oz. Grand Marnier
Shake. Strain into a cocktail glass or a shot-glass.

Mixed drinks made from hard spirits or liqueurs, and served neat in a shot-glass, with a view to being consumed in one swallow. These are sometimes shaken to create a fizzy potion. They are for the drinker in a hurry, or the foolhardy show-off. An example is the politically incorrect B-52.

THE SHRUB

2 quarts Jamaica rum or brandy,
1 pint (or less) lemon juice,
grated rind of 2 to 3 lemons,
4 cups sugar
Soak the lemon rind in the rum for 2 to 3 days. Add the sugar to 1 quart water, and heat until it has dissolved. Mix all the ingredients, strain and bottle. Seal the bottle tightly, and store in a cool place. Serve in a brandy snifter with a slice of orange.

A drink which is made by soaking fruit or peel, traditionally lemons, in liquor, with sugar. An old English idea. The Shrub is kept for no less than a week, and preferably five or six weeks, before being used. The liquor may then be drunk straight, or diluted. Serves 24.

SIDECAR ★

2 oz. cognac or armagnac,
½ oz. lemon juice,
¼ oz. Cointreau,
twist of lemon peel
Shake thoroughly with plenty of cracked ice, and strain into a cocktail glass. Decorate with the lemon peel.

The drinker who invented this cocktail used to travel by sidecar to the Paris bistro which originally made it for him during the First World War. The drink was popularized by Harry's Bar in Paris.

SILK STOCKINGS

1½ oz. white tequila,
2 oz. evaporated milk,
1 oz. crème de cacao,
1 oz. grenadine,
ground cinnamon, and decorate with a cherry

Mix with cracked ice in a blender. Strain into a cocktail glass. Sprinkle with cinnamon and add the cherry.

A very sickly recipe from Mexico.

THE SLING

2 oz. gin,
1 oz. cherry brandy,
1 oz. lemon juice,
soda (optional)

Shake well, and strain into a Highball or Collins glass, with 1 ice cube. Top up with water or soda.

A sweetish long drink, traditionally based on gin, often containing cherry brandy, and sometimes topped with water rather than soda. The basic Gin Sling of *The Savoy Cocktail Book* contains only the spirit, sugar, water, and one lump of ice. The Singapore Sling, from Raffles Hotel, also contains cherry brandy.

SLIPPERY NIPPLE

1 oz. Irish cream liqueur,
1 oz. Sambuca

Shake with ice and strain into a shot-glass.

Another of those risqué names of the 1990s, and a good use for Bailey's.

SLOE COMFORTABLE SCREW

2 oz. vodka,
½ oz. sloe gin,
½ oz. Southern Comfort,
4 oz. orange juice

Pour into Highball glass filled with ice cubes. Stir well. A version containing sloe gin and orange juice is known simply as a Sloe Screw.

This sexy-sounding concoction has given a new life to sloe gin, once the stirrupcup of England's hunting set.

THE SMASH

A shorter **Mint Julep**, usually served in an Old Fashioned glass, and often made with brandy.

2 oz. bourbon or rye,
½ oz. lemon juice,
¼ oz. sugar syrup
Shake well with ice cubes, and strain into a Sour glass.

THE SOUR

★

The most basic of the several classic mixed-drink categories which comprise spirit, citrus, and sugar. It should be sour, and it may be served without any ice or other trimmings in its own stemmed glass, rather like an overgrown aperitif cocktail. The recipe here is for the original: the Whiskey Sour.

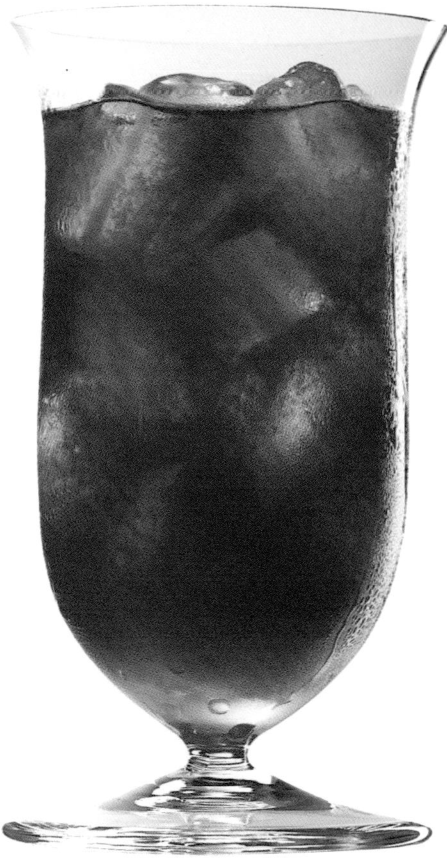

WHISKEY SOUR *THE AGREEABLE ACIDIC TASTE MAKES THE SOUR AN IDEAL PRE-DINNER DRINK.*

SPRITZER

3 oz. chilled dry white wine,
2 oz. soda or Apollinaris water

Pour the wine into a large ballon glass. Add soda or Apollinaris water until two-thirds full. Do not ice.

A revivalist interpretation of the hock-and-seltzer of Lord Byron's day – a mixture which is wonderfully refreshing.

THE STINGER ★

1½ oz. jigger of any spirit (name your poison),
1 oz. white crème de menthe or peppermint schnapps

Shake with cracked ice, and strain into a cocktail glass or serve on the rocks in an Old Fashioned glass.

Brandy is best.

STREGA FLIP

1 oz. Strega,
1 oz. brandy,
2 teaspoons orange juice,
1½ teaspoons sugar syrup,
1 teaspoon lemon juice,
1 egg,
nutmeg

Shake very thoroughly with cracked ice and strain into a cocktail glass. Dust with nutmeg.

The distinctive Italian liqueur is also used to flavor a gin-based Strega Sour.

TENNESSEE

3 oz. rye,
2 tablespoons maraschino,
2 teaspoons lemon juice

Shake with ice cubes, and serve on the rocks in an Old Fashioned glass.

Jack Daniel's might be preferred.

TEQUILA SUNRISE ★

¾ oz. grenadine,
1½ oz. tequila,
4 oz. orange juice

Usually served on the rocks in an Old Fashioned glass although the effect can be better in a large cocktail glass, straight up.

The ingredients are poured straight into the glass, with the grenadine providing the sunrise, but there is disagreement as to which order of elements achieves this best. A Tequila Sunset is made with golden tequila, lemon juice and light honey. A Tijuana Sunrise has Angostura bitters instead of grenadine.

THANKSGIVING COCKTAIL

1 oz. dry gin,
1 oz. dry vermouth,
1 oz. apricot brandy,
a few drops of lemon juice,
1 cherry
Shake with ice cubes, and strain into a cocktail glass. Decorate with the cherry.

To build an appetite for the turkey in November.

TOM COLLINS see The Collins ★

UNION JACK

1½ oz. London Dry gin,
1 tablespoon Crème Yvette
Shake well with crushed ice, and strain into a cocktail glass.

The gin may be English, but the violet-petal liqueur was named after the French actress Yvette Gilbert.

VIA VENETO

1¾ oz. Italian brandy,
2 teaspoons sambuca,
2 teaspoons lemon juice,
1½ teaspoons sugar syrup,
½ egg white
Shake well with crushed ice, and strain into a cocktail glass.

Sambuca Romana must be the preferred brand.

Whiskey Sour see The Sour

WHITE LADY

A generous 2 oz. gin,
½–¾ oz. lemon juice,
¼ oz. triple sec,
½ egg white
Shake very vigorously with ice, and strain into a cocktail glass. In a sweeter version the lemon juice is abandoned in favor of cream and sugar. Some versions abandon the egg white. Others use brandy and crème de menthe.

The name hints at purity, with perhaps a suggestion of seduction ahead. Was this a purportedly "virgin" cocktail during Prohibition? It is said to have been devised by Harry's Bar, in Paris.

WHITE SATIN

♥

A recipe from the Netherlands.

1 oz. Galliano,
1 oz. Tia Maria,
1 oz. heavy cream
Shake well with crushed ice, and strain into a cocktail glass.

XERES

A corruption of Jerez? Surprisingly, it's not.

3 oz. dry sherry,
1–2 dashes of orange bitters,
1–2 dashes of peach bitters
Shake well with ice cubes, and strain into a cocktail glass.

ZOMBIE

"A joke drink," say bartenders in Britain, through their professional guild. No doubt their counterparts elsewhere in the world agree. The object is to get as many different rums as possible into one drink, like students in a telephone booth.

1½ oz. golden rum,
1 tablespoon Jamaica rum,
1 tablespoon light rum,
3 tablespoons lime juice,
1 tablespoon pineapple juice,
1 tablespoon papaya or passionfruit juice,
1½ teaspoons sugar syrup
Shake, or mix in a blender, with a scoop of ice shavings. Serve over more ice in a tall glass. Float one teaspoon of 75% (151 proof) rum on top. Sprinkle with sugar. Decorate with elaborate garnishes.

THE HANGOVER

HOW TO CURE IT

Considering the misery which it causes, the hangover has yielded disappointingly little to serious medical research, but the following remedies do have at least some scientific basis.

❶ If you can think about measures beforehand without spoiling your evening, then the precautionary glass of milk really is worthwhile. It will retard the absorption of alcohol, and protect your stomach against the worst consequent irritations.

❷ If you are prepared to be bored, drink only vodka or one of the other relatively pure continuous-still spirits. The more individualistic pot-still spirits, like brandies and malt whiskies, are more likely to contain traces of toxic higher alcohols. Since no two whiskies or brandies are alike, it is worth experimenting to find one that doesn't hurt.

❸ Some vermouths and digestifs may contain tiny traces of toxic compounds deriving from their plant content, though this is open to argument. The same is held to be true of fortified wines and, to a lesser extent, ordinary wines and beers. Only the latter are likely to be drunk in quantity, but it is worth watching out for labels that bring headaches.

❹ Alcohol causes dehydration because it is a diuretic. So is coffee, which may therefore make you feel worse. Drink water before you go to bed, and leave some handy in case you wake up in the night. Dehydration also causes that trembly feeling.

❺ An irritated stomach may produce acid. That is why antacid patent medicines can be helpful (though caution is advised if they contain aspirin). Mineral waters are alkaline as well as being quenching, so they are doubly useful. Chilled Perrier is excellent, and Kingsley Amis recommends Vichy.

6 Sleep helps the body recover. For the same reason, a tired or unfit drinker is especially vulnerable to hangovers and no two people respond in quite the same way to each different drink.

7 A bath is refreshing, and cleanses the soul.

8 Vitamin C helps the liver detoxify the blood, and B vitamins may be beneficial.

9 Fructose helps the body metabolize alcohol. It also replaces blood sugar, which may be low in the morning. A low level of blood sugar makes you feel weak. Eat bread and honey.

10 Jewish remedy: to combat dehydration, upset stomach, and hunger, drink chicken soup.

11 Hair of the dog: this replaces lost blood sugar, but sets you on the way to another hangover.

FOR THE MORNING AFTER...

BIBLIOGRAPHY / FURTHER READING

Writers being what they are, books have been devoted to many aspects of drink. I have referred to many of them, including my own past works. My brief comments are intended as an indication of style.

ON DRINKS IN GENERAL:

GROSSMAN'S GUIDE TO WINES, BEERS AND SPIRITS
Harriet Lembeck, Scribners

STRAIGHT UP OR ON THE ROCKS – A CULTURAL HISTORY OF AMERICAN DRINK
William Grimes, Simon & Schuster

THE WORLD GUIDE TO SPIRITS
Tony Lord, Macdonald and Jane's, London

ON TYPES OF DRINK:

ABSINTHE – HISTORY IN A BOTTLE
Barnaby Conrad, Chronicle Books

NICHOLAS FAITH'S GUIDE TO COGNAC AND OTHER BRANDIES
Nicholas Faith, Mitchell Beazley

MICHAEL JACKSON'S BEER COMPANION
Michael Jackson, Running Press

MICHAEL JACKSON'S COMPLETE GUIDE TO SINGLE MALT SCOTCH (3RD EDN)
Michael Jackson, Running Press

SAKE
Fred Eckhardt, Eckhardt Publications

SCOTCH WHISKY
David Daiches, Fontana, London

SIMON & SCHUSTER'S POCKET GUIDE TO BEER
Michael Jackson, Simon & Schuster

THE GIN BOOK
John Doxat, Quiller Press

THE MAKING OF SCOTCH WHISKEY
Michael Moss and John Hume, James & James

THE MITCHELL BEAZLEY POCKET WHISKY BOOK
Charles MacLean, Mitchell Beazley, London

THE NEW WORLD GUIDE TO BEER
Michael Jackson, Courage Books

THE SCOTCH WHISKY INDUSTRY RECORD
Charles Craig, Index

THE WHISKIES OF SCOTLAND
R. J. S. McDowall and William Waugh, New Amsterdam Books

THE WORLD ATLAS OF WINE (4TH EDN)
Hugh Johnson, Simon & Schuster

THE WORLD GUIDE TO WHISKEY
Michael Jackson, Running Press

ON MIXED DRINKS:

THE BARTENDER'S BIBLE
Gary Regan, HarperCollins

THE COMPLETE BOOK OF MIXED DRINKS
Anthony Dias Blue, Harper Perennial

THE FINE ART OF MIXING DRINKS
David A. Embury, Doubleday. The most detailed work.

THE SAVOY COCKTAIL BOOK
Harry Craddock, Constable. The bartenders' favorite.

TROPICAL BAR BOOK
Charles Schumann, Stewart Tabori and Chang

INDEX

INDEX OF INGREDIENTS

GENERAL INDEX